Dancing with the Dead

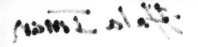

Also by Red Pine/Bill Porter

Travel Writings (as Bill Porter)

South of the Yangtze: Travels through the Heart of China
Finding Them Gone: Visiting China's Poets of the Past
The Silk Road: Taking the Bus to Pakistan
South of the Clouds: Travels in Southwest China
Yellow River Odyssey
Zen Baggage: A Pilgrimage to China
Road to Heaven: Encounters with Chinese Hermits

Chinese Poetry

A Shaman's Lament: Two Poems by Qu Yuan
Cathay Revisited
Written in Exile: The Poetry of Liu Tsung-yuan
The Mountain Poems of Stonehouse
Guide to Capturing a Plum Blossom by Sung Po-jen
In Such Hard Times: The Poetry of Wei Ying-wu
The Collected Songs of Cold Mountain

Chinese Poetry Anthologies

*Poems of the Masters: China's Classic Anthology of T'ang
    and Sung Dynasty Verse*
*The Clouds Should Know Me by Now:
    Buddhist Poet Monks of China* (with Michael O'Connor)

Buddhist, Zen, and Taoist Texts

Dancing
with
the Dead

The Essential

Red Pine
TRANSLATIONS

COPPER CANYON PRESS
PORT TOWNSEND, WASHINGTON

Cover art by Song Boren, from *Guide to Capturing a Plum Blossom.*
Cover design by Gopa & Ted2, Inc.

Copper Canyon Press is in residence at Fort Worden State Park
in Port Townsend, Washington, under the auspices of Centrum.
Centrum is a gathering place for artists and creative thinkers
from around the world, students of all ages and backgrounds,
and audiences seeking extraordinary cultural enrichment.

The Library of Congress has catalogued this record under
LCCN 2022046004.

9 8 7 6 5 4 3 2 FIRST PRINTING

COPPER CANYON PRESS
Post Office Box 271
Port Townsend, Washington 98368
www.coppercanyonpress.org

Contents

DANCING WITH THE DEAD

PREFACE: DANCING WITH THE DEAD

This book is a record of my adventures over the past fifty years in the world of Chinese poetry, a world I never expected to visit, much less make my home.

Whenever I think about this, I can't help but laugh. I never had any interest in Chinese when I was younger, nor in poetry, and certainly not in translation. Then, in the spring of 1970, I applied to Columbia University to study for a PhD in anthropology. Since my only income at the time was the $175 I received every month courtesy of the G.I. Bill, I checked every financial aid box on the application for which I qualified. One of them was for a fellowship funded by the Department of Defense for American citizens studying rare languages—and in 1970 that included Chinese. I had just read a book by Alan Watts titled *The Way of Zen*, and I thought the book made wonderful sense—and it had some Chinese characters in it that I lingered over, wondering how such a writing system was possible. So, I wrote the word *Chinese* and moved on to the next box. Several months later,

I received the surprising news that I'd been awarded the fellowship, and my life changed.

I felt like such a fraud, and it must have showed. The fellowship required attending Intensive Chinese three hours a day, five days a week. The class was taught by an instructor known to anyone who came within her orbit as the "Dragon Lady." The nickname wasn't a joke. When the course began, there were over twenty of us. A month later, we were down to four. Then one day she asked me to stay after class. She said, "Mister Porter, I only teach the best, and you're not good enough. I want you to drop the class." I told her my fellowship required that I take her class, that I couldn't drop it. She said, "I don't care. If you come to class, I'll treat you as if you weren't here." And that was what she did. After a few weeks, the chairman of the East Asian Studies Department intervened. But his intervention only made things worse: she gave me a D for the class, which would have canceled my fellowship. Fortunately, Columbia allowed students to challenge classes for credit, and I was able to replace the D with a B. That was my introduction to Chinese.

Of course, the next year was easier. In fact, it was a pleasure, as I began my study of Classical Chinese. But more significantly, one of the casualties of the Dragon Lady's class introduced me to Master Shouye, a Chinese monk who lived in Chinatown, and I started spending weekends with him at a Buddhist retreat outside the city. Before long, I realized the path to Enlightenment made more sense than a PhD. At the end of the school year, I declined the remaining two years of the fellowship and moved to a monastery in Taiwan.

The monks and nuns had never had a Westerner in their midst, and they didn't know what to do with me. I ended up with a lot of time on my hands. In addition to sutras, I began reading Chinese poetry and discovered the joys of translation—but not right away. The Chinese view of poetry is that it comes from the heart, not the head. It wasn't until I got past the head and found my way to what the Chinese call the "square inch" behind the words, that I finally felt the joy. I hope you will feel it too.

Red Pine
October 28, 2022
On a Train in Taiwan

PUMING

PUMING 普明

No one knows who Puming was or when he produced his *Oxherding Pictures and Verses* 牧牛圖頌. The earliest surviving copy we have was published by Zhuhong in 1609. Despite being one of the most knowledgeable Buddhist monks of his day, Zhuhong didn't know who Puming was, either. The consensus is that he lived during the Song dynasty (960–1278), when woodblock printing began and when three other monks produced similar series: one with five pictures and verses, one with six, and another with ten.

The idea was at least as old as the time of the Buddha. The night of his Nirvana, Sakyamuni told his followers: "Monks, once you are able to keep the precepts, you should prevent your five senses from indulging in the five desires. Be like the herd boy who, staff in hand, watches over his ox and keeps it from ravaging others' sprouts and crops."*

It was a popular metaphor among Zen Buddhists. A typical example concerns a disciple of the ninth-century Zen Master Guishan. One day when Guishan's dharma heir was instructing his disciples, he said, "For more than thirty years, I ate Guishan rice and peed Guishan piss, but I didn't learn any Guishan Zen. All I did was watch a water buffalo. If it left the path and wandered into the weeds, I pulled it back out. If it trampled rice sprouts, I gave it the switch until it

* *Testament Sutra* 遺教經.

learned better. At long last the poor beast understands what I tell it. Now it's turned into a white ox that stays in plain view and never leaves my sight. I can't even drive it away."*

Like the Buddha, Puming used the ox to represent desires associated with our five senses. But being an artist, he saw an opportunity to use image and color to say more. Over the course of ten panels, he shows us the gradual taming of our incarnate desires as a result of the Zen student's use of the rope of meditation and the switch of the precepts. At the same time, he shows us how the dark clouds of our ignorant, deluded mind (our sixth sense) are transformed as well, as the light of the Dharma moon penetrates and finally reveals the emptiness of our thoughts and our world as well as that of our herd boy self. Finally, to all of this, Puming added poems, just to make sure that we saw what he saw and that we realized emptiness is not as empty as some people might think. What a gift!

The first time I saw Puming's series was in D.T. Suzuki's *Manual of Zen Buddhism.* The pictures and verses were so simple yet profound, I spent more time with Puming than I did with the sutra selections. A few years later, in 1980, I came across an actual string-bound copy in Hong Kong. It was published by Saddhaloka, a German monk who lived in the former crown colony. In addition to caring for Vietnamese refugees, he arranged for the reprinting of a number of classic Buddhist texts in limited editions. I carried my

* *Transmission of the Lamp* 傳燈錄, Ch. 9.

copy back to Taiwan as if I had a treasure in my bag and resolved not only to translate the verses but to do what Saddhaloka had done. I used the thousand dollars a friend in America sent me and had a thousand copies printed with handmade paper, bound with the traditional string binding, and sent to my tree-planting poet friends at Empty Bowl in Port Townsend to distribute. Publishing that little string-bound edition and putting it into the hands of friends and strangers gave me a pleasure I had never experienced before. I wanted to do it again, and I did. That was thirty books ago, but Puming and his ox are still with me. The simplest lessons are the hardest to practice, but at least they're easier to keep in mind.

I Untamed

A raging ox with menacing horns
runs away across hills and streams
where black clouds shroud the valleys
who knows what sprouts it tramples

II Taming Begun

Suddenly my rope is through its nose
it tries to run but I use the switch
a willful nature is hard to tame
a boy must pull with all his might

III Restrained

Gradually tamer the ox doesn't bolt
through water and clouds it follows in step
not relaxing his hold on the rope
the herd boy forgets fatigue

IV   Turning Its Head

With constant effort he turns its head
its unruly mind gradually calms down
the herd boy can't let go just yet
he holds the rope or leaves it tied

V Tamed

In willow shade by an ancient stream
the herd boy gives the ox free rein
from dusk's jade sky and sweet grass fields
he leads it home untied

VI Unhindered

Dozing in the open its mind at ease
it no longer needs the rope or switch
the boy sits serene below a pine
expressing his joy with a pastoral tune

[vi] Next to the boy is a rain cape made of barkcloth.

VII With the Current

Beside a willow-lined stream at dusk in spring
the mist-covered grass is lush and sweet
the ox eats and drinks whenever it wants
the boy falls asleep on a rock

VIII Forgetting the Other

The white ox stays in the white clouds now
like the boy it has no cares
the clouds turn white when the moon shines through
the clouds and moon go their own ways

viii The stars are those of the Weaving Maid (Lyra minus Vega) who meets
the Herd Boy once a year on the bridge that spans the Milky Way.

IX Alone in the Light

The ox is gone the herd boy free
one last cloud among the peaks
beneath the moon he claps and sings
one more pass to go

ix The Big Dipper is seen here from the other side of the cosmos.

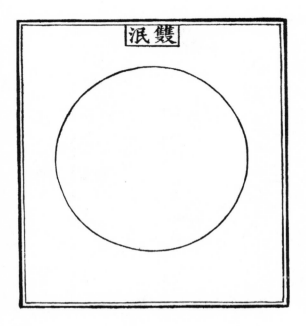

X   Both Gone

Of ox and boy there's no trace
in the light of the moon everything is empty
you who ask what this means
sweet grass and wildflowers surround you

Cold Mountain
& Friends

COLD MOUNTAIN & FRIENDS 寒山與儔

One day in 1974, Abbot Wuming 悟明 called me into the monastery office. He opened a cupboard, reached into a box of books, and handed me one. He said he helped finance the publication and thought I might like it. There was some English in the back, he added—which turned out to be the pirated translations of Burton Watson. On the cover was a picture of two funny-looking guys, one standing with a broom, the other reading a scroll, and both were laughing. The title was *Cold Mountain Poems & Commentary* 寒山詩解. I had seen Cold Mountain's Chinese name before, in Jack Kerouac's *Dharma Bums,* which he dedicated to Hanshan, or Cold Mountain. Suddenly, without any effort on my part, I had his poems. The abbot suggested I try translating a few. And that was what I did, first at Haiming Monastery 海明寺 and later at the house I rented at Bamboo Lake 竹子湖, overlooking Taipei.

Other than Hanshan's status as a hero of the Beat Generation, I had no idea who he was. It turns out he was one of the first Chinese poets to write in a language everyone could understand—including me. Also, unlike the poems of the literati, his weren't meant to impress with their euphony or literary skill but to encourage spiritual practice. And try to find another poet who had as much fun—who not only laughed at others but also at himself. I felt like I had found a friend and a mentor.

It took a while, but I finally got to the end of the poems and thought about publishing my translations of the ones I understood. Attempts to interest publishers went nowhere. Then one day an American knocked on my door. He said he had heard I was translating Hanshan's poems and wondered whether I needed a publisher. The American's name was Mike O'Connor. He was in Taiwan with his wife, who was there working on a degree. He was also a poet and a member of a tree-planting cooperative in Port Townsend that published books on the side. In addition to introducing me to his friends at Empty Bowl, he introduced me to Copper Canyon, another Port Townsend press. Suddenly, I not only had a home for Puming but one for Cold Mountain as well. Sometimes the gods just can't help smiling.

As for who Hanshan was, that was another thing that set him apart. We know nothing, not even his real name. He was an enigma. Still, despite such anonymity, there are things he says in his poems that allow us to create a likely story. He was born around 730 and probably on the western edge of the Yellow River floodplain in the town of Handan (poem 28). He must have been educated and well-connected, as he mentions visiting the imperial palace in Chang'an (48) and riding on horseback in the royal hunting preserve north of the capital (101). In half a dozen poems he suggests he was lame (271), perhaps the result of a riding injury. That would have prevented him from holding any significant post, as a sound body was one of the job requirements. Given the number of poems set in Luoyang (63), that was probably where he settled. It was the Tang dynasty's eastern capital, and it would have been easy for him to support himself there as a tutor. But an event occurred there that changed his life—and the lives of everyone else in China: the An Lushan Rebellion, which broke out in 755 and resulted in the death of nearly half the population. When the rebels made Luoyang their capital, Hanshan's impairment would have been overlooked, and he would have been pressed into service in some capacity. Two years later, Luoyang was retaken by imperial forces, and those who had served the rebels were imprisoned or executed. Hanshan fled south, leaving his family—and his name—behind. Whether it was a well-off life (134, 137) or he was just getting by (21, 31) is hard to say. Some poems sound biographical, others idyllic.

And so, Hanshan began a new life alone, one involving spiritual cultivation—both Daoist (267) and Buddhist (82)—and he sought out places of seclusion (79). In that regard, he could not have done better than Tiantaishan 天台山. It was famous for its Daoist hermits. Hanshan, though, chose the Buddhist sanctuary of Guoqing Temple 國清寺 at the foot of the mountain—especially when he met its two resident bodhisattvas, Fenggan 豐干 and Shide 拾得.

Fenggan (Big Stick) was a tall monk who showed up at the monastery one day accompanied by a tiger. And Shide (Pickup) was an orphan Fenggan heard crying in the bushes on a nearby trail and brought back to the temple, where he ended up working in the kitchen. That was him with the broom on the cover of the book the abbot gave me.

When Hanshan was thirty (131), which would have been around 760, he established a residence of his own at the mouth of a cave twenty kilometers south of Guoqing. He then spent the rest of his life going between the two places, depending on the whim or the weather (44). Meanwhile, he wrote poems on trees and rocks and monastery walls.

As for how the poems found their way into our hands, a local official reportedly heard about Hanshan and ordered his aides to collect them. That's one story. A more likely one is that sometime before he died in 841, the Daoist Xu Lingfu 徐靈府 collected the poems after meeting Hanshan on Tiantaishan when Hanshan was over a hundred—an age to which Hanshan himself attests (195).

Of course, all of this is just conjecture, and Hanshan, no doubt, would have found it amusing that anyone cared. In any case, we have the poems, and within two hundred years of someone collecting them, they became part of China's literary firmament. The Song-dynasty prime minister Wang Anshi (d. 1086) wrote twenty verses titled "In Imitation of Hanshan and Shide." And when the poems of these nascent dharma bums appeared in woodblock editions in 1189 and again in 1201, their stature was assured.

Not everyone, though, smiled at the thought. Despite the praise of some of China's most famous poets—or perhaps because of it—literary critics have never stopped reminding people that Hanshan and Shide were not really poets and their poems not really poems (144, 283). I can hear Hanshan and Shide laughing. No doubt, you soon will, too.

from *The Collected Songs of Cold Mountain*

4

Looking for a refuge
Cold Mountain will keep you safe
a faint wind stirs dark pines
come closer the sound gets better
below them sits a gray-haired man
chanting Daoist texts
ten years unable to return
he forgot the way he came

5

My mind is like the autumn moon
clear and bright in a pool of jade
nothing can compare
what more can I say

16

People ask the way to Cold Mountain
but roads don't reach Cold Mountain
even in summer the ice doesn't melt
sunny days the fog is too dense
how did something like me arrive
our minds are not the same
if they were the same
you would be here

18

I spur my horse past ruins
ruins move a traveler's heart
the old parapets high and low
the ancient graves great and small
the shuddering shadow of a tumbleweed
the steady sound of evergreens
but what I lament are the common bones
unnamed in the records of immortals

21

My parents stayed busy enough
I don't envy others' gardens and fields
my wife clacks away at her loom
our baby gurgles and coos
I clap and urge the flowers to dance
or prop up my chin and listen to birds
who comes to commend me
woodcutters sometimes stop by

[18] The Chinese plant evergreens at gravesites as reminders of long life.

26

Since I came to Cold Mountain
how many thousand years has it been
accepting fate I fled to the woods
I pass the time contemplating what I will
no one visits the cliffs
forever obscured by clouds
soft grass serves as a mattress
my quilt is the dark blue sky
happy with a rock for a pillow
I don't care if Heaven and Earth change

28

This maid is from Handan
my singing has the lilt
make use of my refuge
there's still more to this song
you're drunk don't talk of going
stay until the sun is high
where you sleep tonight
my brocade quilt fills a silver bed

[28] Handan is a city on the western edge of the Yellow River floodplain known for its female entertainers. My guess is it was Hanshan's hometown.

31

A recluse lives under thatch
before his gate carts and horses are rare
the forest is secluded but partial to birds
the stream is wide and home to fish
with his son he picks wild fruit
with his wife he hoes between rocks
what does he have in his house
a shelf lined with nothing but books

40

An old lady who lives to the east
got rich a few years ago
before poorer than me
she mocks my poverty now
she laughs that I'm behind
I laugh that she's ahead
neither of us can stop laughing
from the east and from the west

43

A white crane carries a bitter flower
a thousand miles without resting
bound for the peaks of Penglai
with this for his provision
not yet there his feathers break off
far from the flock he sighs
returning to his old nest
his wife and children don't know him

44

I prefer a secluded place
but sometimes I go to Guoqing
to call on Venerable Fenggan
or visit Master Shide
but I go back to Cold Cliff alone
observing an unspoken agreement
I follow a stream that has no spring
the spring is dry but not the stream

[43] The white crane is a Daoist symbol for transcendence. Penglai is the name of an island inhabited by Daoist immortals.

[44] Guoqing Temple was where Hanshan lived when not at Hanyan (Cold Cliff). Fenggan was an older monk who lived at Guoqing, and Shide worked in the kitchen. The "stream" refers to karma, the "spring" to its origin: the Three Poisons of ignorance, desire, and anger.

48

Beneath high cliffs I live alone
the clouds and mist last all day
inside my hut it might be dim
but my mind is free of noise
I passed through a golden gate in a dream
my spirit returned when I crossed a stone bridge
I left behind what weighed me down
my dipper on a branch click clack

53

Once I reached Cold Mountain
I stayed for thirty years
recently visiting family and friends
most had left for the Yellow Springs
slowly dying like a sputtering candle
or surging on like a passing stream
today facing my solitary shadow
suddenly both eyes filled with tears

[48] The golden gate was at the entrance to the imperial palace in Chang'an. The stone bridge is still there at the entrance of Guoqing Temple. Someone once gave the hermit Xu You a gourd dipper. He took one drink with it and left it hanging on a pine branch, clacking in the wind.

[53] The Yellow Springs are the destination of the dead, named for the sulfurous rock found where the earth opens up.

63

In Luoyang so many girls
on a spring day show off their charms
in groups picking roadside flowers
sticking them high in their hair
high in their hair the flowers wind round
people look and they snicker
they're not for attracting new lovers
but to show husbands at home

65

Girls play in the fading light
wind fills the road with perfume
their skirts embroidered with butterflies of gold
their hair adorned with ducks of jade
their maids attired in red chiffon
their eunuchs in purple brocade
watching is someone who lost his way
white temples and a trembling heart

79

I chose a secluded place
Tiantai says it all
gibbons howl and the stream fog is cold
a view of the peak adjoins my front gate
I covered my hut with leaves
I made a pool by channeling a spring
glad at last to put everything down
picking ferns I pass the years left

82

Spring water is pure in an emerald stream
moonlight white on Cold Mountain
still your thoughts and your spirit becomes clear
focus on emptiness and the world calms down

89

Anger is a fire in the mind
it can burn up a forest of merit
if you plan to travel the bodhisattva path
forbearance keeps anger away

[79] The last line refers to Boyi and Shuqi, who vowed to survive on ferns rather than eat the food of a realm ruled by an unrighteous king.

[82] A summary of the *zhi-guan* 止觀 "still and focus" meditation technique promoted by Zhiyi, founder of Guoqing Temple and Tiantai Buddhism.

101

I recall the days of my youth
off hunting near Pingling
an envoy's job wasn't my wish
I didn't think much of immortals
I rode a white horse like the wind
chasing hares I loosed a falcon
suddenly now with no home
who will show an old man pity

107

My scrolls are filled with the poems of masters
my jugs overflow with the wine of sages
my favorite pastime is watching buffalo calves
when I sit I don't go far
and when my thatched eaves are soaked with dew
and moonlight lights my crockery sill
I sip a couple of cups
and intone a verse or two

[101] The plateau of Pingling, north of Xianyang, the old capital of the Qin dynasty, was a royal hunting preserve during the Tang dynasty.

[107] It was common for poor people to break off the mouths of large earthen pots to use as window frames.

131

Born thirty years ago
I've traveled countless miles
along rivers where the green rushes swayed
to the frontier where the red dust swirled
I've made elixirs and tried to become immortal
I've read the classics and written odes
and now I've retired to Cold Mountain
to lie in a stream and wash out my ears

134

Yesterday was so long ago
the scene so worthy of sighs
above was a path of peach trees and plums
below was an iris-lined shore
and someone was wearing fine silk
and kingfisher feathers in our house
we saw each other and tried to talk
we looked but couldn't speak

[131] When the third-millennium-BCE hermit Xu You was offered the throne, he walked down to a nearby stream and washed out his ears, lest they be contaminated by such talk.

[134] Blue-green kingfisher feathers were used by women of means to paste on their eyebrows.

137

Last night I dreamed I went home
I saw my wife at her loom
she stopped the shuttle as if in thought
then raised it with hardly enough strength
I called and she turned to look
she looked but didn't know me
I guess we had been apart too many years
and my temples weren't their old color

144

When stupid people read my poems
they don't understand and sneer
when average people read my poems
they reflect and say they're deep
when gifted people read my poems
they react with full-face grins
when Yang Xiu saw *young woman*
one look and he understood *mystery*

[144] Yang Xiu was adept at riddles. Here he sees the characters 少 (young) and 女 (woman) and combines them to form 妙 (mystery).

172

I'm poor alas and I'm sick
a man without friends or kin
there's never any rice in the pot
and the steamer is always lined with dust
my thatched hut doesn't keep out the rain
and my caved-in bed hardly holds me
no wonder I'm so haggard
all these cares wear a man down

180

I reached Cold Mountain and all cares stopped
no idle thoughts remained in my head
nothing to do I write poems on rocks
and trust the current like an unmoored boat

183

They laugh at me *hey farm boy*
your face is a little thin
your hat isn't high enough
and your belt is far too tight
it's not that I don't know the trends
when you're broke you can't catch up
one day I'll be rich
and stick a stupa on my head

195

Chronically ill about out of years I'm over a hundred
face tanned head white I'm content with mountain life
cloth robe pulled tight I accept what karma brings
why would I envy the clever ways of others

197

Is there a self or not
is this me or not
this is what I contemplate
sitting undecided below a cliff
between my feet green grass grows
on my head red dust settles
I have even seen pilgrims
leave offerings by the bier

199

On ancient rocks are ancient tracks
below towering cliffs is a clearing
always bright when the bright moon shines
no need to ask directions

[197] "Red dust" refers to sensations of the material world.

203

Above Cold Mountain the moon shines alone
in the clear sky it illuminates nothing at all
precious heavenly priceless jewel
buried in the skandhas submerged in the body

204

Down to the stream to watch the jade flow
or back to the cliff to sit on a boulder
resting on nothing my mind is like a cloud
what do I need in the faraway world

218

People who meet Cold Mountain
they all say he's crazy
his face isn't worth a glance
his body is wrapped in rags
they don't understand what I say
what they say I don't dare
here's a message for those in the future
come to Cold Mountain sometime

---

[203] The skandhas are five aspects wherein we search in vain for a self: form, sensation, perception, memory, and consciousness.

220

As long as I lived in the village
people thought I had no peer
yesterday down in the city
I was even sized up by the dogs
some objected my pants were too tight
others said my shirt was too long
if hawks were only cross-eyed
sparrows would dance like lords

225

The ocean's water is boundless
its fishes and dragons by the billion
everyone eating someone else
busy stupid lumps of flesh
as long as the mind doesn't stop
delusions rise like mist
the moon of our nature is clear and bright
in the open it shines without limit

234

Cold Mountain speaks these words
as if he were a madman
he tells people what he thinks
thus he incurs their wrath
but an honest mind means honest words
an honest mind holds nothing back
what will you do at death's door
who is that jabbering fool
the road to the grave is dark
and karma holds the reins

244

All my life too lazy to work
favoring the light to the heavy
others take up a career
I hold on to a sutra
a scroll with nothing inside
I show everyone I meet
for every illness it has a cure
it saves with whatever works
once your mind isn't busy
wherever you are it's alert

255

People search for roads through the clouds
but cloud roads leave no tracks
the peaks are high and sheer
the streams are wide and deep
ridges rise in front and back
clouds stretch east to west
I'll tell you where cloud roads are
cloud roads are in the sky

267

Ever since I left home
I've developed an interest in yoga
contracting and stretching the four-limbed Whole
attending intently the six-sensed All
wearing ragged clothes winter and spring
eating coarse fare morning and night
I'm hard on the trail even now
hoping to meet a buddha

[255] Cloud roads are said to lead to the land of the immortals.

271

I recall twenty years ago
my slow steps ending at Guoqing
the residents of Guoqing Temple
all said Cold Mountain is a fool
why did they think I was a fool
they concluded I couldn't reason
but I don't know myself yet
so how could they
I bowed and didn't bother asking
why ask anyway
some of them reproached me
that I understood
even though I didn't answer
I came out ahead

275

I've always admired friends of the Way
friends of the Way I've always cherished
meeting someone with a dried-up spring
or welcoming someone talking Zen
talking about the unseen on a moonlit night
searching for the truth until dawn
when all trace of our countless schemes disappears
and we finally see who we are

282

From the top of a towering peak
the view extends forever
I sit here unknown
the lone moon lights Cold Spring
in the spring there is no moon
the moon is in the sky
I sing this solitary song
a song in which there is no Zen

283

Mister Wang the Graduate
laughs at my poor prosody
I don't know a wasp's waist
much less a crane's knee
I can't keep my flat tones straight
all my words come helter-skelter
I laugh at the poems he writes
a blind man's songs about the sun

[283] The location of flat and inflected tones in Chinese poetry was standardized during the Tang. Hanshan ignored such rules, with the Chinese of this poem being an example.

293

Dressed in sky-flower clothes
wearing tortoise-hair shoes
clutching rabbit-horn bows
they hunt the ghosts of delusion

304

Deep in the mountains
there's always a breeze
no need for a fan
the cool air comes through
lit by the moon
surrounded by clouds
I sit here alone
a white-haired old man

307

Whoever has Cold Mountain's poems
is better off than someone with sutras
write a few on your screen
and read them from time to time

[293] Cold Mountain pokes fun at those who use delusion to rid themselves of delusions. People with cataracts see flowers in the sky, people with wild imaginations see hair on a tortoise, and people with dim vision mistake a rabbit's ears for horns.

[307] Three-section folding screens were used for privacy and to divide spaces in a dwelling.

FENGGAN

3

Whenever Cold Mountain stops to visit
or Pickup pays his usual call
we talk about the mind or moon
or wide-open space
since reality has no limit
anything real includes it all

4

Actually there isn't a thing
much less any dust to wipe away
who can master this
doesn't need to sit there stiff

[4] This poem refers to the poetry competition to become Zen's Sixth Patriarch. Shenxiu wrote: "Our body is the Bodhi Tree / the mind is a propped-up mirror / always keep it clean / don't let it gather dust." Huineng, who became the Sixth Patriarch, countered, "Bodhi isn't some kind of tree / this mirror doesn't have a stand / our buddha nature is forever clear / where do you get this dust?"

SHIDE

16

My poems are poems alright
but some people call them gathas
gathas or poems what's the difference
readers should be careful
take your time going through
don't think they're so easy
use them for your practice
they'll make it much more fun

22

Cold Mountain is Cold Mountain
and Pickup is Pickup
Big Stick knows our faces
but fools don't recognize us
they don't see us when we meet
when they look we aren't there
if you wonder what's the reason
it's the power of doing nothing

[16] Gathas were originally four-line poems used to summarize prose sections
of a sutra, and they later became stand-alone poems.

23

I was Pickup from the first
no accidental name
Cold Mountain is my brother
I have no other kin
our two minds are alike
we can't follow worldly ways
if you want to know our ages
count the times the Yellow River has cleared

29

Silver stars dot the beam
green silk marks the weight
buyers move it forward
sellers move it back
never mind the other's anger
as long as you prevail
when you die and meet Old Yama
up your butt he'll stick a broom

[23] The Yellow River is the world's muddiest river, carrying over three times more mud than the runner-up—the Colorado.

[29] This is a description of a handheld scale. Yama is Judge of the Dead and Lord of the Underworld.

49

Woods and springs make me smile
no kitchen smoke for miles
clouds rise up from rocky ridges
cascades tumble down
a gibbon's howl is a song indeed
a tiger's roar is transcendent
pine wind sighs so softly
birds discuss singsong
I walk the winding streams
and climb the peaks alone
sometimes I sit on a boulder
or lie and gaze at trailing vines
but when I see a distant town
all I hear is noise

STONEHOUSE

STONEHOUSE 石屋

If you have never heard of Stonehouse, you aren't alone. Few people have, even in China. Back in the early 1980s when I was translating the poems of Hanshan, one of the editions I was using included the poems of a Buddhist monk. When I reached the end of Cold Mountain's poems, there was Stonehouse waiting for me. I couldn't believe my good fortune. I was captivated, and yet I couldn't find anyone in Taiwan who had heard of him. Undeterred, after I finished with Cold Mountain's poems, I translated those of Stonehouse as well and, in 1986, published them in a string-bound edition with my friends at Empty Bowl and later in a regular trade edition, first with Mercury House, then with Copper Canyon. Of all the poems I have translated, those of Stonehouse are still my favorite. I'm not alone. W.S. Merwin told me he kept them on his bedside table for years.

Unlike with Cold Mountain, we actually know something about Stonehouse. He was born in 1272, not far from where the Yangzi empties into the East China Sea, and his family was sufficiently well-off that he was educated. He even planned to take the exams that might have led to a career as an official. But his life among his educated peers did not last long enough for him to find out. When he was twenty, he quit his studies and became a novice monk. After three years of training, he was formally ordained and given the name Qinggong 清珙. But the name by which he became known wasn't Qinggong. It was Stonehouse (Shiwu 石屋). It was the name of a famous cave at the edge of the town where he grew up, and it was not uncommon for people to be referred to by the name or some feature of their hometown.

Being a young monk, Stonehouse did what many young monks did and still do: he sought instruction elsewhere, first with Gaofeng 高峯 on Tianmushan, west of Hangzhou, then with Ji'an 及安 on Chuzhou's Langyashan, west of Nanjing. When Ji'an was later asked to take over as abbot of a monastery near Huzhou 湖州, Stonehouse joined him, at least for a while. Eventually, Stonehouse decided he preferred mountains, and he found one to his liking a day's hike to the south. It was called Xiamushan 霞幕山 (Sunset Screen Mountain). The year was 1312, and he was forty. For thirty-three of the next forty years, he lived at the summit, leaving only once, for a seven-year period, to become abbot of a monastery sixty kilometers to the east.

In the spring of 1352, in recognition of his fame among Buddhist monks, the empress presented Stonehouse with a robe woven from golden thread. She must have known he was ill. He died later that autumn. His cremated remains were placed inside a stupa near his old hut, and the information I have summarized above is from its inscription.

After publishing his poems in that first string-bound edition, I began thinking about visiting the place where he wrote them. But it wasn't until five years later that I had the chance. I was gathering material south of the Yangzi for a series of English-language programs for a Hong Kong radio station in the fall of 1991 and traveling with my Empty Bowl friends Finn Wilcox and Steve Johnson. When we finally reached Huzhou, I knew Stonehouse's mountain was south of town, but I didn't know exactly where. I figured we would buy tickets on the next bus headed in that general direction and wing it. But while we were waiting, a crowd of onlookers gathered, and the stationmaster suggested we wait in his office. While our host left to get us some tea, I looked at his walls. On one of them was a topographic map of the entire county. It took me less than thirty seconds to find Xiamushan. The name was still the same. When the stationmaster returned, I pointed to the map. Not only did he refund our tickets, he hired a taxi to take us there.

It was slow going, but once the driver learned which mountain was Xiamushan, we started up a narrow dirt road, and he managed to keep his battered Polish Škoda sedan going far beyond where sense would have suggested he stop. Finally, just below the summit, a chain and a set of blockhouse buildings barred our way. While our driver parked his car, we climbed over the chain and started up a trail that led the rest of the way to the summit.

A few minutes later, we were there—not that we had a better view. The bamboo was so high, we couldn't see past it. All we could see was a metal tower and a big metal dish and a cement bunker, from which half a dozen soldiers came running with rifles pointed in our direction. As they surrounded us, the base commander came puffing up the trail from one of the blockhouses below. I explained that we were looking for traces of a monk who had lived on the mountain six hundred years earlier—which in China isn't such a silly thing to say as it sounds. I showed him the Empty Bowl edition of my translations, which included the Chinese text. His eyes widened, and he smiled. He waved the soldiers away, pulled out his machete, and led us straight into the bamboo.

Half an hour later, we reemerged at a small farmstead and open vistas. The commander said that before the telecommunication base was built, the farmhouse was the only structure on the mountain. As we approached, a farmer appeared in the doorway. He said the place was originally a small Buddhist temple whose monks had been forced to leave during the Cultural Revolution. In the six hundred years since Stonehouse lived there, the place hadn't changed much. The roof was now covered with tiles instead of thatch, and the walls were made of piled rocks instead of mud and woven bamboo slats. But the dirt floor was the same dirt floor, and the spring that formed the pond Stonehouse called Sky Lake still flowed from the rocks in back.

The farmer invited us inside for a cup of tea. He lived there alone, he said. His children had grown up, and his wife had moved down to the village at the foot of the mountain, where life was easier. He had been living at the summit by himself, he said, for the past twenty years. Like Stonehouse, he didn't have much to say. Neither did we. All we could do was smile.

from *The Mountain Poems of Stonehouse*

1

I made my home west of the Cha
where water fills Sky Lake and the moon fills the stream
strangers are frightened by the mountain's heights
but once they arrive they know the trail
dried snail shells on rock walls
fresh tiger tracks in the mud
I leave my door open when spring days get longer
when paulownias bloom and thrushes call

6

Movement isn't right and stillness is wrong
cultivating no thought means confusion instead
the Patriarch didn't have no mind in mind
any thought at all means trouble
a hut facing south isn't so cold
chrysanthemums beside a fence perfume the dusk
as soon as a drifting cloud starts to linger
the wind blows it past the vines

[1] The Cha River flowed past Xiamushan, through Huzhou, then into Lake Taihu. Sky Lake is the pond formed by the spring behind Stonehouse's hut.

[6] Bodhidharma was China's First Patriarch of Zen.

16

A white-haired Zen monk with a hut for my home
my robe has been torn into rags by the wind
down by the stream I rake leaves for the stove
after a frost I wrap a mat around the orange tree
ultimate reality isn't created
ready-made koans aren't worth a thought
I sit by my open window all day
looking at mountains without lowering the shade

21

A human life lasts one hundred years
but which of us gets them all
precarious as a hut made of thatch
or a leaking boat in a storm
mediocre monks are pathetic
would-be masters sadder still
the world's empty ways aren't what they were
some days I shut my old door tight

[16] Since this is the only mention of an orange tree, I assume Stonehouse was too late with the mat. Citrus trees don't do well along this part of the Yangzi. During the Song dynasty, Zen masters started using examples of earlier masters' enlightenment (*gong'an* in Chinese, *koan* in Japanese), or phrases culled from such accounts, as means to awaken their disciples.

25

I chose high cliffs far from a market
a half-closed gate overgrown with weeds
where is the pauper who isn't deferential
or the rich man who isn't vain
emergency loans don't come without strings
to dispel delusions you need a quiet place
clouds too say mountains are better
returning at night they ease the solitude

28

A friend of seclusion arrives at my gate
greeting we pardon our lack of decorum
manes of white hair more or less tied
monk robes somehow covering our frames
embers of leaves at the end of the night
howl of a gibbon announcing the dawn
sitting on cushions wrapped in quilts
words forgotten we finally meet

31

This body lasts about as long as a bubble
may as well let it go
things don't always go as we wish
who can step back doesn't worry
we blossom and fade like flowers
gather and part like clouds
I forgot the world a long time ago
relaxing all day in a teetering hut

33

Day after day I let things go
why worry about tomorrow today
the four afflictions are hard to predict
wealth and honor don't last
lakeside villas swallowed by vines
deserted promenades along the river
these are things anyone can see
but few are willing to consider

[33] The four afflictions: birth, illness, old age, and death. The villas and promenades would have been in nearby Huzhou, where the Cha River joins Taihu, one of China's largest freshwater lakes.

36

I was a Zen monk who didn't know Zen
so I chose the woods for the years I had left
a robe of patches hanging from my body
a belt of bamboo wrapped around my waist
mountains and streams explain the Patriarch's meaning
flower smiles and bird songs reveal the hidden key
sometimes I sit on a flat-topped rock
cloudless afternoons once a month

48

Examine the patterns of transient existence
the outcome of a game of chess isn't fixed
a monk in the mountains needs to be free
people in the dust grow old unaware
windblown tea smoke floats above my bed
stream-borne petals fill the pond outside
with thirty-six thousand days
why not spend a few staying still

[36] The transmission of Zen is said to have begun when the Buddha held up a flower and Kasyapa smiled.

50

I'm a poor but happy follower of the Way
whatever happens takes care of my needs
last night the west wind blew down an old tree
at daybreak firewood covered the ground
windblown white silk graced the red scarps
dewdrop pearls adorned the green cliffs
my survival has always depended on what's present
why should I exhaust myself making plans

51

You know very well yet seem not to know
speechless like a dunce or a fool
you keep still while storms flatten mountains
not a thought moving for ten thousand years
with ears you hear the wind in the trees
with no mind you respond like a pond to the moon
but don't think you alone understand
this is something anyone can do

52

The shame of dumb ideas is suffered by the best
but the absence of intelligence means a fool for sure
claiming an object is nothing but illusion
unaware getting rich is simply chance
the leaves in the stream move without a plan
the clouds in the valley drift without design
I close my eyes and everything is fine
I open them again because I love mountains

56

There isn't much time in this fleeting life
why spend it running in circles
when the kitchen is bare I go look for yams
when my robe needs a patch I consider lotus leaves
I've put down the deer tail and stopped giving sermons
my long-forgotten sutras are home to silverfish
I pity those who wear a monk's robe
with so many goals and attachments

[56] The Chinese yam, *Dioscorea bulbifera,* grows on vines and is a food of last resort. In English, it is often referred to as the "air potato." The deer tail refers to the animal-hair wands abbots used as a symbol of authority. Stonehouse would have held one when he was abbot of Fuyuan Monastery in Pinghu 平湖. His sermons there appear in *The Zen Works of Stonehouse.*

57

Followers of the Way are done with reason
wherever they look is the light of the mind
somewhere peach trees are blooming
their petals perfume the stream
deep grass is bliss for a snake
sunshine is butterfly heaven
one day I heard a woodcutter mention
a lean-to in the clouds

60

Reasoning comes to an end
a thought breaks in the middle
all day nothing but time
undisturbed all year
clouds come and go on a deserted mountain
in a clear sky the moon is a lonesome O
even if yoga or alchemy worked
it couldn't match knowing Zen

[57] The reference to Tao Yuanming's "Peach Blossom Spring" is about
tracing peach petals upstream to an unspoiled world. This poem likely
recounts the first time Stonehouse heard about Xiamushan.

66

A hoe supplies a living
there's plenty of water and wood all year
mountains to relax my eyes
nothing to cause me trouble
even when mist soaks through my thatch roof
and moss covers the steps on the trail
accepting conditions I conserve my strength
no need to arrange a thing

70

A thatch hut in a bamboo grove
beyond the dusty world
a pond before the door
mountains out every window
a tea-stove black with soot
a hemp robe streaked with dirt
if I didn't follow the King of Emptiness
how did I end up here

[70] The Buddha is the King of Emptiness.

76

A thatch hut is lonely on a new fall night
with white peas in flower and crickets calling
mountain moon silver evokes an old joy
suddenly I've strolled west of the summit

77

Slopes of fiddleheads terraces of tea
one tree of pink among the white
of all the seasons spring is the best
a mountain home then is especially fine

78

Someone asked what year I arrived
I had to think before the answer came
the peach tree I planted outside my door
has flowered in spring twenty times

85

I plant winter melon then aubergine
I wear myself out staying alive
but someone who wants a decent kitchen
needs to have a garden nearby

[76] Referring to the midautumn full moon, when family members in China gather and stay up all night.

86

Will the porridge or rice ever end
will the sun or moon ever rest
either way it's no concern of mine
so many fantasies rise in vain

88

It's something no one can force
besides knowing it's there there's nothing to know
seeing the moon above a flowering plum
it's too late to look at the blossoms

89

What's gone is already gone
and what hasn't come needs no thought
right now I'm writing a right-now line
the plums are ripe and gardenias in bloom

90

Three or four naps every day
still don't exhaust all my free time
I circle the jade bamboo a few times
and gaze at distant mountains beyond the pines

91

The flux of attachments is easy to stop
but it's hard all at once to end love and hate
I laugh at the mountain for towering so high
and the mountain mocks me for being so puny

94

Old and exhausted I'm truly lazy
no folded hands at dawn anymore
to those who visit I have nothing to say
their trek to my hut is such a waste of effort

95

Old through and through I'm utterly lazy
a hundred fantasies all turn to ashes
but the moment a friend arrives
inescapable feelings force me up

96

There's no dust to sweep on a mountain
guests have to knock before I open the door
after a snowfall the setting moon slips through the eaves
the shadow of a plum branch comes right to the window

97

My hut is two maybe three mats wide
surrounded by mountains on every side
my bamboo bed couldn't hold a cloud
I shut the door before sunset

98

Why do my Zen friends choose smoke and vines
this life of mine isn't hard
gardenias below the cliff perfume the trees
shoots in my garden form furrows of green

100

Ten thousand fantasies and schemes have ceased
all that I've known and seen has vanished
my two fine ears are no good at all
I sit past the cockcrow and the evening bell

101

My home in the mountains is like a tomb all day
barren of even one worldly thought
although I eat food and wear clothes
it's as if I were dead just not yet cremated

[98] Line 1 refers to the incense smoke and koan riddles of monastic life.

102

There's a snag in front like a standing man
and a ridge in back like a curling wave
regarding me there's nothing to say
it's the road through the clouds that tricks friends here

104

A hundred years slip by unnoticed
eighty-four thousand cares dissolve in the quiet
a mountain image shimmers on sunlit water
snowflakes swirl above a glowing stove

107

Trying to become a buddha is easy
but ending delusions is hard
how many frosty moonlit nights
have I sat and felt the cold before dawn

108

Stripped of conditions my mind is still
emptied of existence my nature is calm
often at night my windows turn white
the moon and the stream come right to my door

[108] Windows were covered with oil paper.

109

Work with no mind and all work stops
no more joy and no more sorrow
but don't think no mind means you're done
there is still the thought of no mind

112

Head of white hair shoulders all bones
I've lived in a hut more years than I can count
my shorts have no drawstring my pants no legs
and half of my robe is missing

116

No one else sees what I see clearly
no one else knows what I know well
I recall one misty day last fall
a gibbon came by and stole two pears

117

Half the window pine shadow half the window moon
a solitary cushion a solitary monk
sitting cross-legged after midnight
when a moth puts out the altar lamp

118

Not one care in mind all year
I find enough joy every day in my hut
and after a meal and a pot of strong tea
I sit on a rock by the pond and count fish

123

A few trees in bloom radiant red
a pond in spring rippling green
a monk with eyes that see beyond Zen
doesn't have to be dead to use them

129

My hut isn't quite ten feet on a side
surrounded by pines bamboo and mountains
an old monk hardly has room for himself
much less for a visiting cloud

131

Our time is confined to one hundred years
but which of us gets them all
hundred-year-olds die too
the only difference is sooner or later

137

People say our everyday mind isn't our buddha nature
I say our buddha nature is simply our everyday mind
afraid no one will do any work
they teach grinding iron rods to make needles

145

From outside my round pointed-roof hut
who would guess how big it is inside
all the worlds in the universe are there
with room to spare for a meditation cushion

150

Now that I'm old nothing disturbs me
I'm asleep on my cot before the sun sets
dreaming and wondering who I am
until the crescent moon lights the plum blossoms

151

After meditation I chant a Cold Mountain poem
after dinner I brew some valley-mist tea
and when a feeling lingers I can't express
I cross the ridge with a basket to gather vine buds

157

I sit and meditate in the quiet and dark
where nothing comes to mind
I sweep in front when the west wind is done
I make a path for the moonlight

158

Jade-winged plum blossoms perfumed trees
pond-washed vegetables floating stalks of green
if the silk-clad young lords knew about this
they would move into the wilds for sure

166

Spring is gone summer is gone and autumn was cool
days are like a shuttle and nights are getting long
people fill their time with idle talk and chatter
how often do they stop and think

169

People say there's always time to practice
if not this life there's next life
but headed for five thousand kalpas below
they won't be back anytime soon

[169] A kalpa is the length of time between a world's creation and its destruction.

174

Cold Mountain has a line
my mind is like the autumn moon
I have a line of my own
my mind outshines the autumn moon
not that the autumn moon isn't bright
but once it's full it fades
how unlike my mind
forever round and bright
as for what the mind is like
what more can I say

181

Letting go means letting everything go
buddhahood has to go too
each thought becomes a demon
each word invites more trouble
eat and drink what karma brings
pass your days in freedom
use the Dharma for your practice
lead your ox to the mill

[174] Line 2 quotes Cold Mountain's poem 5. The last line is also the last line of that poem.

[181] This poem alludes to the six desires, including thinking. See Puming's *Oxherding Pictures and Verses.*

from *Poems for Zen Monks**

6   Four Mountain Postures

Walking in the mountains
unconsciously trudging along
grab a vine
climb another ridge

Standing in the mountains
how many dawns become dusk
plant a pine
a tree of growing shade

Sitting in the mountains
zigzag yellow leaves fall
nobody comes
close the door and make a big fire

Lying in the mountains
pine wind through the ears
for no good reason
beautiful dreams are blown apart

---

* Written when Stonehouse interrupted his stay on Xiamushan to serve as abbot of Fuyuan Temple in Pinghu, east of Huzhou, 1331–1338.

6 Buddhist precepts governing behavior stipulated what to avoid while walking, standing, sitting, or lying down.

20 For Monk Jiu on His Way to Honor the Patriarchs

Everyone possesses bones made of gold
why go around worshipping stupas
Zen monk Jiu from Danyang you're crazy
leaving East Zhejiang in late spring

32 For Attendant Zhen

How many years have you practiced Zen
three perfect shouts didn't knock you down
off you went seeking further instruction
now you're back for a slap in the face

41 For Monk Mao

To be a god or buddha is easy
the hardest thing to be is a monk
getting older and thinner and seldom resting
if it's not firewood or water it's temple work

[20] In poem 77 of his *Mountain Poems,* Stonehouse says spring was the best time of year where he was living, which was in East Zhejiang. So why would anyone hit the trail to visit the stupas of the Zen patriarchs a thousand kilometers away?

43 For Monk Qin

Find a switch to use in your practice
to drive daydreams and lethargy away
late at night when the clouds are gone
the sky is like water and the moon is alone

44 For Monk Ying

Braving spring cold you found my hidden door
your robe still flecked with snow
sit down and show me what others are saying
but open your eyes before you unroll your scroll

61 No Enemies

Your eyes empty oceans your spirit rides clouds
a monk among monks your thoughts are unique
who were you once and who are you now
go easy on others when you have the chance

LAOZI

LAOZI 老子

If there is one Chinese book people in the West are likely to have heard of, it's the *Daodejing* 道德經. Next to the *Bible* and the *Bhagavad Gita,* the "Book of the Way and Virtue" is the most translated book in the world. Containing a mere 5,000 "words," it hangs like a ripe fruit within reach of anyone who likes their philosophy simple yet profound.

Written at the end of the sixth century BCE by a man known as Laozi, the "Old Master," the *Daodejing* is not only a philosophical text, it's a book of poems, China's oldest book of poems, eighty-one verses about the *Dao,* or "Way." In teaching people how they should live their lives, China's ancient philosophers each had their own take on the Dao. Laozi's Dao was not the same as that of Confucius or the authors of such texts as the *Yijing.* Laozi extolled failure, not success. His favorite metaphor in conveying this teaching was the moon. Later Daoists used the moon's two conjoined phases, its *yin* and its *yang,* to summarize their understanding of the Dao. But for Laozi, who lived in the excessively *yang* society of one of the world's early civilizations, it was the *yin* that needed our attention. Rather than being like the full moon, destined to wane, better to be like the new moon, destined to grow brighter. And so he advised cultivating what is empty but inexhaustible, what doesn't try to be full, the light that doesn't blind, the crescent soul, the dark womb, the dark beyond dark, what doesn't die.

Despite the Dao's elusiveness, Laozi says we can approach it through *De* 德, or "Virtue." In his commentary on the *Daodejing,* Yan Lingfeng 嚴靈峰 says, "Virtue is the manifestation of the Way. The Way is what Virtue contains. Without the Way, Virtue would have no power. Without Virtue, the Way would have no appearance." The philosopher Han Fei 韓非 put it simpler: "Virtue is the Way at work."

Laozi saw people chasing the light, wanting more, and hastening their own end; hence, he taught them the Virtues of the dark instead of the light, the female instead of the male, less instead of more, weakness instead of strength, inaction instead of action. Hence, concerning "the manifestation of the Way," he advised cultivation that "involves neither effort nor the thought of effort" (38). It was such a simple philosophy, but not for those determined to do something.

The man who wrote these poems in praise of darkness and of no effort was born in 604 BCE, near the ancient city of Huaiyang 淮陽 in the middle of what we now call China. Other than that, the only thing we know about him is that he became keeper of the Zhou dynasty's royal archives at its capital of Luoyang 洛陽, and in 516 BCE he was visited there by Confucius. Confucius came to inquire about ritual and music—in a word, *harmony.* A stele still marks the spot, which was where Laozi's house once stood. Laozi told his young visitor, "The ancients you admire have been in the ground a long time. Those among them who were wise rode in carriages when times were good and slipped quietly away when times were bad. I advise you to get rid of your excessive pride and ambition. This is all I have to say to you."

Not long after this, Laozi decided it was time to take his own advice. He left Luoyang and headed west. A few days later, he arrived at Hanguguan Pass 函谷關. According to the early historian Sima Qian 司馬遷, the warden of the pass was a Daoist named Yin Xi 尹喜, who recognized Laozi as a sage and asked for instruction. Laozi gave him the *Daodejing* and continued traveling west, never to be heard from again.

As you might imagine, during the 2,500 years since Laozi gave Yin Xi the *Daodejing,* the text has appeared in a variety of editions, each incorporating its own set of variants. Lately, we have also been blessed—or cursed—with the discovery of copies dating back as early as 300 BCE that provide even more variants to choose from. For translators, working on this text can be like walking across a minefield or through a candy store. For me it was both, being captivated by new possibilities but also having to reconsider perfectly good interpretations.

Over the centuries, some of China's greatest thinkers have devoted themselves to studying and reflecting on this text, and no Chinese would think of reading the *Daodejing* without the help of at least one of their line-by-line or verse-by-verse explanations. So that English readers would not be at a disadvantage, I have included a selection of their comments in what follows.

from *Laozi's Daodejing*

I

The way that becomes a way
is not the Immortal Way
the name that becomes a name
is not the Immortal Name
no name is the maiden of Heaven and Earth
name is the mother of all things
thus in innocence we see the beginning
in passion we see the end
two different names
for one and the same
the one we call dark
the dark beyond dark
the door to all beginnings

DU ERWEI (d. 1987) says, "*Dao* originally meant 'moon.' The *Yijing* [hexagrams 42 and 52] stresses the bright moon, while Laozi stresses the dark moon." (*Laozide yueshen zongjiao*)

CONFUCIUS (d. 479 BCE) says, "The Dao is what we can never leave. What we can leave isn't the Dao." (*Zhongyong* 1)

HESHANGGONG (fl. 130) says, "What we call a way is a moral or political code, while the Immortal Way takes care of the spirit without effort and brings peace to the world without struggle. It conceals its light and hides its tracks and can't be called a way. As for the Immortal Name, it's like a pearl inside an oyster, a piece of jade inside a rock: shiny on the inside, dull on the outside."

CHENG ZHU (d. 1144) says, "Sages don't reveal the Way, not because they keep it secret, but because it can't be revealed. Hence their words are like footsteps that leave no tracks."

SU CHE (d. 1112) says, "The ways of kindness and justice change but not the way of the Dao. No name is its body. Name is its function. Sages embody the Dao and use it in the world. But while entering the myriad states of being, they remain in non-being."

WANG BI (d. 249) says, "From the infinitesimal all things develop. From nothing all things are born. When we are free of desire, we can see the infinitesimal where things begin. When we are subject to desire, we can see where things end. 'Two' refers to 'maiden' and 'mother.'"

CAO DAOCHONG (d. 1115) says, "'Two' refers to 'innocence' and 'passion,' or in other words, stillness and movement. Stillness corresponds to nonexistence. Movement corresponds to existence. Provisionally different, they are ultimately the same. Both meet in darkness."

HANSHAN DEQING (d. 1623) says, "Laozi's philosophy is all here. The remaining five thousand words only expand on this first verse."

Underlying this verse is the concern during Laozi's day with the correspondence, or lack thereof, between name and reality. We give things a name in an effort to distinguish them. The problem arises when things change, but their names don't.

3

Bestowing no honors
keeps people from fighting
prizing no treasures
keeps people from stealing
displaying no attractions
keeps people from making trouble
thus the rule of the sage
empties the mind
but fills the stomach
weakens the will
but strengthens the bones
by keeping the people from knowing or wanting
and those who know from daring to act
the sage governs them all

Su CHE says, "Bestowing honors embarrasses those who don't receive them to the point where they fight for them. Prizing treasures pains those who don't possess them to the point where they steal them. Displaying attractions distresses those who don't enjoy them to the point where they cause trouble. If people aren't shown these things, they won't know what to want and will cease wanting."

WANG ZHEN (fl. 809) says, "Sages empty the mind of reasoning and delusion, fill the stomach with loyalty and honesty, weaken the will with humility and compliance, and strengthen the bones with what we already have within ourselves."

WANG BI says, "Bones don't know how to make trouble. It's the will that creates disorder. When the mind is empty, the will is weak."

LU NONGSHI (d. 1102) says, "The mind knows and chooses, while the stomach doesn't know but simply contains. The will wants and moves, while bones don't want but simply stand there. Sages empty what knows and fill what doesn't know. They weaken what wants and strengthen what doesn't want."

YAN ZUN (d. 24 BCE) says, "They empty their mind and calm their breath. They concentrate their essence and strengthen their spirit."

HUANG YUANJI (d. 1874) says, "Sages purify their ears and eyes, put an end to dissipation and selfishness, embrace the one, and empty their mind. An empty mind forms the basis for transmuting cinnabar by enabling us to use our *yang* breath to transform our *yin* essence. A full stomach represents our final form, in which our *yang* breath gradually and completely replaces our *yin* essence."

WEI YUAN (d. 1856) says, "The reason the world is in disorder is because of action. Action comes from desire. And desire comes from knowledge. Sages don't talk about things that can be known or display things that can be desired. This is how they bring order to the world."

LIU JING (d. 1074) says, "This verse describes how sages cultivate themselves in order to transform others."

6

The valley spirit that doesn't die
we call the dark womb
the dark womb's mouth
we call the source of Heaven and Earth
it's like gossamer silk
yet it can't be exhausted

THE *SHANHAIJING* 山海經 says, "The Valley Spirit of the Morning Light is a black and yellow, eight-footed, eight-tailed, eight-headed animal with a human face" (9). The *Shanhaijing*'s "valley spirit" is the moon, which runs ahead of the sun the last eight days of its thirty-day cycle, lags behind the first eight days, and faces the sun during its eight days of glory. For the remaining days, it's too close to the sun to be visible. Like other ancient cultures, the Chinese viewed the moon as the embodiment of the female element of creation.

WANG BI says, "The valley is what is in the middle, what includes nothing, no form, no shadow, no obstruction. It occupies the lowest point, remains motionless, and does not decay. All things depend on it for their development, but no one sees its shape."

YAN FU (d. 1921) says, "Because it is empty, we call it a 'valley.' Because there is no limit to its responsiveness, we call it a 'spirit.' Because it is inexhaustible, we say it 'doesn't die.' These three are the virtues of the Dao."

SU CHE says, "A valley is empty but has form. A valley spirit is empty but has no form. What is empty and has no form is not alive. So how can it die? 'Valley spirit' refers to its virtue. 'Dark womb' refers to its capacity. This womb gives birth to the ten thousand things. We call it 'dark' because we see it give birth but not how it gives birth."

HESHANGGONG says, "The valley is what nourishes. Those able to nourish their spirit do not die. 'Spirit' refers to the spirits of the liver, lungs, heart, kidneys, and spleen. 'Dark' refers to Heaven. In a person, this means the nose, which links us with Heaven. 'Womb' refers to Earth. In a person, this means the mouth, which links us with Earth. The breath that passes through our nose and mouth should be finer than silk and barely noticeable, as if it weren't actually present. It should be relaxed and never strained or labored."

WU CHENG (d. 1333) says, "The empty valley is where spirits dwell, where breath isn't exhausted. Who relaxes their breath increases their vitality. Who strains it soon expires."

HANSHAN DEQING says, "Purposeful action leads to exhaustion. The Dao is empty and acts without purpose. Hence, it can't be exhausted."

SONG CHANGXING (fl. 1700) says, "The valley spirit, the dark womb, the source of Heaven and Earth all act without acting. Just because we don't see them doesn't mean they don't exist."

LIU JING says, "It's like the silk of a silkworm or the web of a spider: hard to distinguish and hard to grab. But then, it isn't humankind who uses it. Only the spirit can use it."

LIEZI (c. 400 BCE) says, "What creates life is not itself alive." (*Liezi* 1.1)

9

Instead of pouring in more
better stop while you can
making it sharper
won't help it last longer
rooms full of treasure
can never be safe
the vanity of success
invites its own failure
when your work is done retire
this is the Way of Heaven

THE *HOUHANSHU* 後漢書 says, "What Laozi warns against is 'pouring in more.'"

XUNZI (d. 238 BCE) says, "In the ancestral hall of Duke Huan, Confucius reports watching an attendant pour water into a container that hung at an angle. As the water level approached the midpoint, the container became upright. But when the attendant went beyond the midpoint, it tipped over, the water poured out, and after it was empty, it resumed its former unbalanced position. Seeing this, Confucius sighed, 'Alas! Whatever becomes full becomes empty.'" (*Xunzi* 28)

LU DONGBIN (d. 1016) says, "This is about the basics of cultivation. These are the obstacles when you first enter the gate."

LIU SHILI (fl. 1200) says, "Since fullness always leads to emptiness, avoid satisfaction. Since sharpness always leads to dullness, avoid zeal. Since gold and jade always lead to worry, avoid greed.

Since wealth and honor encourage excess, avoid pride. Since success and fame bring danger, know when to stop and where lies the mean. You don't have to live in the mountains and forests or cut yourself off from human affairs to enter the Way. Success and fame, wealth and honor are all encouragements to practice."

YAN ZUN says, "To succeed without being vain is easy to say but hard to practice. When success is combined with pride, it's like lighting a torch. The brighter it burns, the quicker it burns out."

WANG ZHEN says, "To retire doesn't mean to abdicate your position. Rather, when your task is done, treat it as though it were nothing."

HESHANGGONG says, "Excessive wealth and desire wearies and harms the spirit. The rich should help the poor, and the powerful should aid the oppressed. If, instead, they flaunt their riches and power, they are sure to suffer disaster. Once the sun reaches the zenith, it descends. Once the moon becomes full, it wanes. Creatures flourish then wither. Joy turns to sorrow. When your work is done, if you do not step down, you will meet with harm. This is the Way of Heaven."

HUANG YUANJI says, "You need a raft to cross a river. But once across, you can forget the raft. You need to study rules to learn how to do something. But once you know how, you can forget the rules."

II

Thirty spokes converge on a hub
but it's the emptiness
that makes a wheel work
pots are fashioned from clay
but it's the hollow
that makes a pot work
windows and doors are carved for a house
but it's the spaces
that make a house work
existence makes a thing useful
but nonexistence makes it work

HESHANGGONG says, "Ancient carts had thirty spokes in imitation of the lunar number."

LI RONG (fl. 670) says, "It's because the hub is empty that spokes converge on it. Likewise, it's because the minds of sages are empty that the people turn to them for help."

CHENG XUANYING (b. 608) says, "A cart, a pot, and a house can hold things because they are empty. How much more disciples who empty their minds."

WU CHENG says, "All these things are useful. But without an empty place for an axle, a cart can't move. Without a hollow place in the middle, a pot can't hold things. Without spaces for doors and windows, a room can't admit people or light. But these three examples are only metaphors. What keeps our body alive is the existence of breath within us. And it is our empty, nonexistent mind that produces breath."

SONG CHANGXING says, "Here the Great Sage teaches us to understand the source by using what we find at hand. Doors refer to the mouth and nose. Windows refer to the ears and eyes."

ZHANG DAOLING (d. 157) says, "When ordinary people see these things, they only think about how they might employ them for their own advantage. When sages see them, they see in them the Dao and are careful in their use."

HANSHAN DEQING says, "Heaven and Earth have form, and everyone knows they're useful. But people don't know their usefulness depends on the emptiness of the Way. We also have form and think ourselves useful but are unaware that our usefulness depends on our empty, shapeless minds. Thus, existence has its uses, but real usefulness depends on nonexistence. Nonexistence, though, doesn't work by itself. It needs the help of existence."

HUANG YUANJI says, "What's beyond form is the Dao. What has form are tools. Without tools we've no means to grasp the Dao. Without the Dao there's no place for tools."

XUE HUI (d. 1541) says, "At the end of this verse, Laozi mentions both existence and nonexistence, but his intent is to use existence to show that nonexistence is more valuable. Everyone knows existence is useful, but no one pays attention to the usefulness of nonexistence."

In the Yellow River region where the *Daodejing* was written, people carved their houses out of the loess hillsides.

18

When the Great Way disappears
we meet kindness and justice
when reason appears
we meet great deceit
when the six relations fail
we meet obedience and love
when the country is in chaos
we meet upright officials

SONG CHANGXING says, "It isn't the Great Way that leaves humankind and goes into hiding. It's humankind that leaves the Great Way and replaces it with kindness and justice."

SU CHE says, "When the Great Way flourishes, kindness and justice are at work. Only after the Great Way disappears, do kindness and justice become visible."

WANG ANSHI (d. 1086) says, "The Way hides in formlessness. Names arise from discontent. Hiding in formlessness, the Great Way reveals no difference between great and small. When names arise from discontent, we get distinctions such as kindness, justice, reason, and so forth."

HESHANGGONG says, "When the kingdom enjoys peace, no one thinks about kindness, and the people are free of desire. When the Great Way prevails, kindness and justice vanish, just as the stars fade when the sun appears."

MENCIUS (d. 289 BCE) says, "Kindness means dwelling in peace. Justice means taking the right road." (*Mencius* 4A.10)

HANSHAN DEQING says, "Reason is what the sage uses to order the kingdom. It includes the arts, measurements, and laws. In the High Ages, people were innocent, and these were unknown. In the Middle Ages, people began to indulge their feelings, and rulers responded with reason. Once reason appeared, the people responded with deceit."

WANG BI says, "The six relations are between father and son, elder and younger brother, husband and wife. When these six are harmonious, the country governs itself, and there is no need for obedience, love, or honesty."

WANG PANG (d. 1076) says, "In a virtuous age, obedience and love are considered normal. Hence, no one is called obedient or loving. Now, when someone is obedient or loving, we praise them. This is because the six relations are no longer harmonious. When peace prevails, everyone is honest. How can there be honest officials?"

CHENG XUANYING says, "When the realm is at peace, loyalty and honesty are nowhere to be seen. Innocence and virtue appear when the realm is in chaos."

LI RONG says, "During the time of the sage emperors Fu Xi and Shen Nong, there was no mention of officials. It was only during the time of the despots Jie and Zhou that we hear of ministers like Guan Longfeng and Bi Gan."

ZHUANGZI (d. 286 BCE) says, "When springs dry up, fish find themselves in puddles, spraying water on each other to keep each other alive. Better to be in a river or lake and oblivious of each other." (*Zhuangzi* 6.5)

28

Recognize the male
but hold on to the female
and be the world's maid
being the world's maid
don't lose your Immortal Virtue
not losing your Immortal Virtue
be a newborn child again
recognize the pure
but hold on to the base
and be the world's valley
being the world's valley
be filled with Immortal Virtue
being filled with Immortal Virtue
be a block of wood again
recognize the white
but hold on to the black
and be the world's guide
being the world's guide
don't stray from your Immortal Virtue
not straying from your Immortal Virtue
be without limits again
a block of wood can be split to make tools
sages make it their chief official
a master tailor doesn't cut

HANSHAN DEQING says, "To recognize the Way is hard. Once you recognize it, holding on to it is even harder. But only by holding on to it can you advance on the Way."

MENCIUS says, "The great person does not lose their child heart." (*Mencius* 4B.12)

WANG DAO (d. 1532) says, "Sages see 'that' but hold on to 'this.' 'Male' and 'female' mean hard and soft. 'Pure' and 'base' mean noble and humble. 'White' and 'black' mean light and dark. Hard, noble, and light have their uses, but hard comes from soft not hard; noble comes from humble not noble; and light comes from dark not light. Hard, noble, and light are the secondary forms and farther from the Way. Hence, sages return to the original: a block of wood. A block of wood can be made into tools, but tools cannot be made into a block of wood. Sages are like blocks of wood, not tools. They are the chief officials, not functionaries."

CHENG XUANYING says, "What has no limits is the Dao."

CONFUCIUS says, "A great person is not a tool." (*Lunyu* 2.12)

ZHANG DAOLING says, "Who makes tools loses sight of the Way."

SONG CHANGXING says, "Before a block of wood is split, it can take any shape. Once split, it can't be round if it's square or straight if it's curved. Laozi tells us to avoid being split. Once we are split, we can never return to our original state."

BAODING says, "When I first began butchering, I used my eyes. Now I use my spirit and follow the natural lines." (*Zhuangzi* 3.2)

WANG PANG says, "Who uses the Dao to tailor leaves no seams."

40

The Dao moves the other way
the Dao works through weakness
the things of this world come from something
something comes from nothing

LIU CHENWENG (d. 1297) says, "Once things reach their limit, they have to go back the other way."

WEI YUAN says, "The Dao moves contrary to how most people look at things."

ZHAO ZHIJIAN 趙志堅 (fl. eighth century) says, "To go back the other way means to return to the root. Those who cultivate the Dao ignore the twigs and look for the root. This is the movement of the Dao—to return to where the mind is still and empty and actions soft and weak. The Dao, however, does not actually come or go. It never leaves. Hence, it cannot return. Only what has form returns. 'Something' refers to breath. Before things have form they have breath. Heaven and Earth and the ten thousand things are born from breath. Hence, they all come from something. 'Nothing' refers to the Dao. Breath comes from the Dao. Hence, it comes from nothing. This is the movement of the Dao."

WANG ANSHI says, "The reason the Dao works through weakness is because it is empty. We see it in Heaven blowing through the Great Void. We see it on Earth sinking into the deepest depths."

HANSHAN DEQING says, "People only know the work of working. They don't know that the work of not working is the greatest work of all. They only know that everything comes from something. They don't know that something comes from nothing. If they knew that something came from nothing, they would no longer enslave themselves to things. They would turn, instead, to the Dao and focus on their spirit."

HESHANGGONG says, "The ten thousand things all come from Heaven and Earth. Heaven and Earth have position and form. Hence, we say things come from something. The light and spirit of Heaven and Earth, the flight of insects, the movement of worms, these all come from the Dao. The Dao has no form. Hence, we say things come from nothing. This means the root comes before the flower, weakness comes before strength, humility comes before conceit."

LI RONG says, "'Something' refers to Heaven and Earth. Through the protection of Heaven and the support of Earth, all things come into being. 'Nothing' refers to the Dao. The Dao is formless and empty, and yet it gives birth to Heaven and Earth. Thus, it is said, 'Emptiness is the root of Heaven and Earth. Nothingness is the source of all things.' Those who lose the Dao don't realize where things come from."

SU CHE says, "As for 'the things of this world,' I have heard of a mother giving birth to a child. But I have never heard of a child giving birth to its mother."

WANG BI says, "Everything in the world comes from being, and being comes from nonbeing. If you would reach perfect being, you have to go back to nonbeing."

47

Without going out your door
you can know the whole world
without looking out your window
you can know the Way of Heaven
the farther people go
the less they know
thus do sages know without traveling
name without seeing
and succeed without trying

ZHUANGZI says, "Who takes Heaven as their ancestor, Virtue as their home, the Dao as their door, and who escapes change is a sage." (*Zhuangzi* 33.1)

HESHANGGONG says, "Those who are sages understand others by understanding themselves. They understand other families by understanding their own. Thus, they understand the whole world. Humankind and Heaven are linked to each other. If the ruler is content, the breath of Heaven will be calm. If the ruler is greedy, Heaven's breath will be unstable. The sage does not have to ascend into the sky or descend into the depths to understand Heaven or Earth."

WANG BI says, "Events have a beginning. Creatures have a leader. Roads diverge, but they also lead back. Thoughts multiply, but they all share one thing. The Way has one constant. Reason has one principle. Holding on to the ancient Way, we are able to master the present. Although we live today, we can understand the distant past. We can understand without going outside. If we don't understand, going farther only leads us farther astray."

SU CHE says, "The reason the sages of the past understood everything without going anywhere was simply because they kept their natures intact. People let themselves be misled by things and allow their natures to be split into ears and eyes, body and mind. Their vision becomes limited to sights, and their hearing becomes limited to sounds."

WANG PANG says, "If we wait to see before we become aware and wait to become aware before we know, we can see ten thousand different views and still be blind to the reason that binds them all together."

LI XIZHAI (fl. 1167) says, "Those who look for Heaven and Earth look for forms. But Heaven and Earth can't be fathomed through form, only through truth. Once we realize truth is right here, it doesn't matter if we close our door. For those who are wise, knowledge isn't limited to form. Hence, they don't have to go anywhere. Name isn't limited to matter. Hence, they don't have to look anywhere. Success isn't limited to action. Hence, they don't have to do a thing."

CHENG XUANYING says, "'Without traveling' means to know without depending on previous or external experience. 'Without seeing' means to know that everything is empty and that there is nothing to see. 'Without trying' means to focus the spirit on the tranquillity that excels at making things happen."

67

The world calls me great
great but useless
it's because I am great I am useless
if I were of use
I would have remained small
but I possess three treasures
I treasure and uphold
first is compassion
second is austerity
third is reluctance to excel
because I am compassionate
I can be valiant
because I am austere
I can be extravagant
because I am reluctant to excel
I can be chief of all tools
if I renounced compassion for valor
austerity for extravagance
humility for superiority
I would die
compassion wins every battle
and outlasts every attack
what Heaven creates
let compassion protect

HESHANGGONG says, "Laozi says the world calls his virtue 'great.' But if his virtue were great in name alone, it would bring him harm. Hence, he acts foolish and useless. He doesn't distinguish or differentiate. Nor does he demean others or glorify himself."

WANG BI says, "To be useful is to lose the means to be great."

SU CHE says, "The world honors daring, exalts ostentation, and emphasizes progress. What the sage treasures are patience, frugality, and humility, all of which the world considers useless."

HANSHAN DEQING says, "'Compassion' means to embrace all creatures without reservation. 'Austerity' means not to exhaust what one already has. 'Reluctance to excel' means to drift through the world without opposing others."

WANG ANSHI says, "Through compassion, we learn to be soft. When we're soft, we can overcome what is hard. Thus, we can be valiant. Through austerity, we learn when to stop. When we know when to stop, we're always content. Thus, we can be extravagant. Through reluctance to excel, we are surpassed by no one. Thus, we can be chief of all tools. Valor, extravagance, and superiority are what everyone worries about. And because they do, they're always on the verge of death."

LIU SHIPEI (d. 1919) says, "To be chief of all tools means to be the chief official." See also verse 28.

WU CHENG says, "Compassion is the chief of the three treasures. The last section mentions only compassion because it includes the other two. All people love a compassionate person as they do their own parents. Hence, those who attack or defend with compassion meet no opposition."

80

Imagine a small state with a small population
let there be labor-saving tools
that aren't used
let people consider death
and not move far
let there be boats and carts
but no reason to ride them
let there be armor and weapons
but no reason to employ them
let people return to the use of knots
and be satisfied with their food
and pleased with their clothing
and content with their homes
and happy with their customs
and let there be another state so near
people hear its dogs and chickens
and live out their lives
without making a visit

EMPEROR HUANGDI (d. 2600 BCE) says, "A great state is *yang*. A small state is *yin*."

SU CHE says, "Laozi lived during the decline of the Zhou dynasty, when artifice flourished and customs suffered, and he wished to restore its virtue through doing nothing. Hence, at the end of his book he wishes he had a small state to try this on. But he never got his wish."

HESHANGGONG says, "When sages govern great states, they think of them as small states and are frugal in the use of resources. When the people are many, sages think of them as few and are careful not to exhaust them."

HU SHI (d. 1962) says, "With the advance of civilization, the power of technology is used to replace human labor. A cart can carry a thousand pounds, and a boat can carry a hundred passengers. These are 'labor-saving tools.'"

WANG ANSHI says, "When the people are content with their lot, they don't concern themselves with moving far away or with going to war."

THE *YIJING JICI* 易經繫辭 says, "Earlier rulers used knots in their government. Later sages introduced writing."

WU CHENG says, "People who are satisfied with their food and pleased with their clothing cherish their lives and don't tempt death. People who are content with their homes and happy with their customs don't move far away. They grow old and die where they were born."

CHENG XUANYING says, "They are satisfied with their food because they taste the Way. They are pleased with their clothing because they are adorned with Virtue. They are content with their homes because they are content wherever they are. And they are happy with their customs because they soften the glare of the world."

CAO DAOCHONG says, "Those who do their own farming and weaving don't lack food or clothes. They have nothing to give and nothing to seek. Why visit others?"

81

True words aren't beautiful
beautiful words aren't true
the good aren't eloquent
the eloquent aren't good
the wise aren't learned
the learned aren't wise
sages accumulate nothing
but the more they do for others
the greater their existence
the more they give to others
the greater their abundance
the Way of Heaven
is to help without harming
the Way of the Sage
is to act without struggling

HANSHAN DEQING says, "At the beginning of this book, Laozi says the Dao can't be put into words. But are its 5,000-odd characters not words? Laozi waits until the last verse to explain this. He tells us that though the Dao itself includes no words, by means of words it can be revealed—but only by words that come from the heart."

SU CHE says, "What is true is real but nothing more. Hence, it isn't beautiful. What is beautiful is pleasing to see but nothing more. Hence, it isn't true. Those who focus on goodness don't try to be eloquent, while those who focus on eloquence aren't good.

Those who have one thing that links everything together have no need of learning. Those who keep learning don't understand the Dao. The sage holds on to the one and accumulates nothing."

HESHANGGONG says, "True words are simple, not beautiful. The good cultivate the Dao, not the arts. The wise know the Dao, not facts. Sages accumulate virtue, not wealth. They give their wealth to the poor and use their virtue to teach the unwise. Like the sun or moon, they never stop shining."

SONG CHANGXING says, "People only worry that their own existence and abundance are insufficient. They don't realize that helping and giving to others does them no harm and benefits them instead."

CAO DAOCHONG says, "The wealth that comes from giving generously is inexhaustible. The power that arises from not accumulating is boundless."

WU CHENG says, "Help is the opposite of harm. Wherever there's help, there's harm. But when Heaven helps, it doesn't harm, because it helps without helping. Action is the start of struggle. Wherever there's action, there's struggle. But when sages act, they don't struggle, because they act without acting."

JIAO HONG says, "The previous 5,000 words all explain 'the Dao of not accumulating,' what Buddhists call 'nonattachment.' Those who empty their minds on the last two lines will grasp most of Laozi's text."

WANG ZHEN says, "The last line summarizes all the words of the previous eighty verses. It doesn't focus on action or inaction but simply on action that doesn't involve struggle."

SONG BOREN

Song Boren 宋伯仁

When I first began my studies of Chinese, one of the many things I wondered about was why the Chinese held plum blossoms in such high regard. Twenty years later, I finally found out why when I came across a book by Song Boren titled *Guide to Capturing a Plum Blossom* 梅花喜神譜.

I was in South China's cultural capital of Hangzhou a week before the tanks rolled through Tiananmen Square in June of 1989. After interviewing hermits in the mountains south of Xi'an, I was working my way down the coast and back to Taiwan and was browsing in the only bookstore in Hangzhou that sold old books. On a shelf with other dusty survivors of the Cultural Revolution, I found a string-bound copy of the 1928 edition of Song's *Guide.* I was captivated by the pictures and bought the store's only copy. Once I returned to Taiwan, I started going through the book and soon realized the poems that accompanied the pictures were beyond my reach. Up until then, my translations were limited to the more accessible work of Chinese Buddhists. These were by an unknown thirteenth-century official. I gave the book to my friend Lo Ch'ing 羅青, which turned out to be a fortuitous decision.

Lo Ch'ing had studied art with the last emperor's cousin, whom the Nationalists brought to Taiwan should they ever need their own claimant to the throne, in case the republican form of government didn't work out. Lo Ch'ing had heard of Song Boren's *Guide* but had never seen a copy. Surprised by our good fortune, we agreed to enjoy the book together. Every Wednesday for the next four months, we sat down on the tatamis in Lo Ch'ing's tea room, surrounded ourselves with piles of dictionaries, dynastic histories, anthologies, and compendia of all sorts, and spent the morning working our way through five or six poems and as many pots of tea.

As a result of our joint efforts, I was able to make rough translations into English. But before I had time to polish them sufficiently for publication, I put them aside to finish a book about the hermits I had interviewed, then to embark on a series of journeys in China that involved the production of more than a thousand radio programs, and finally to move back to America. It wasn't until 1994 that I was able to pick up the plum book again.

While I was readying my translations for publication, I looked for articles about Song's book and was amazed that no one had paid attention to such a treasure—at least not in print. It was the world's earliest-known printed book of art, first published in 1238. Although there are no extant copies of that first printing, there is a single surviving copy of the second printing—made in 1261 from the same woodblocks—in the Shanghai Museum. The pictures that follow are from that edition.

The most likely reason for the disappearance of early copies is that when the Mongols completed their conquest of China in 1276, the mixture of Chinese nationalism and aesthetics displayed—or referenced—in the *Guide* became treasonous, and Song's book vanished from public notice until the Chinese reclaimed the throne and established the Ming dynasty in 1368.

As for its author, other than his name, we know next to nothing. All we know is that he was born in Huzhou, on the shore of one of China's largest freshwater lakes, at the beginning of the thirteenth century, a century before Stonehouse showed up in the same town. After passing the civil service exam, he was appointed to supervise the salt trade along the Grand Canal.

In presenting his book to the public, Song wrote this: "I painted the flower from the unfolding of its buds to the falling of its petals. I painted more than 200 portraits, and after eliminating those that were too staid or too frail, I was left with 100 distinct views. To each, I then added an old-style poem, and I titled the result *Guide to Capturing a Plum Blossom* because it's about capturing the spirit of the plum flower."

Fortunately, Song's book appeared just as the technology of printing that began with Buddhist sutras in the ninth century was extended to works of literature and art in the twelfth and thirteenth centuries. It was not only the world's first printed book of art, it was the first printed book that combined art with poetry. By reimagining something as simple as a plum blossom and linking the resulting images with touchstones of the Chinese psyche, it opened a door to a secret garden. Nearly eight hundred years later, its scent is still as fresh as it was then.

蓓蕾四枝

雪岩

麥眼

南枝發岐穎
當思漢光武

崆峒占歲登
一飯能中興

from *Guide to Capturing a Plum Blossom*

1 Wheat Eyes

A southern branch erupts with buds
unmarked means a year of plenty
Han Guangwu comes to mind
restoring the throne with a meal

A southern branch feels the warmth of spring first. The Chinese still look to the plum tree for the first sign of spring and even examine its buds to predict the coming season of growth among plants in general. It was from "buds" that the career of Emperor Guangwu began. The year he was born, nine ears appeared on a single stalk of corn in his district, and his mother named him Xiu, meaning "grain flower." Later, when he was put in charge of a granary, he sold wheat and millet at discounted prices and gained a large following among the oppressed. In 25 CE, he toppled the usurper Wang Mang, restored the Han dynasty, and ascended the throne as emperor.

丁　香

小蘖一十六枝

藥性貴溫涼　胡爲辛且烈

無與桂附徒　天資更趍熱

5   Cloves

Herbs that warm and cool are prized
so why this fire and spice
not following cinnamon's lead
ordained by Heaven to make things hot

Cinnamon is an important ingredient in herbal tonics designed to revitalize the body without overstimulating it. As such, its effects are described as both warming and cooling, and its application in Chinese medicine is extensive. The major use of cloves is in treating "cold" illnesses that require something hotter than cinnamon. The Chinese view illness as an imbalance between *yin* and *yang,* and treatment as a restoration of that balance. While reminding the reader of the beneficial effects of cinnamon, Song uses the cloves here to suggest the inflexibility or excess of some policy or person supported by the emperor.

古文錢

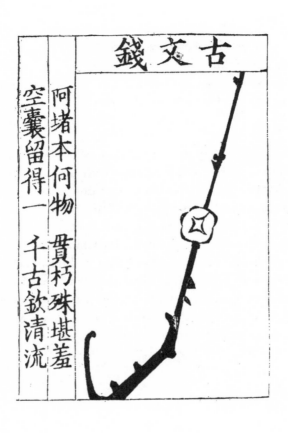

阿堵本何物　貫朽殊堪羞

空囊留得一　千古欽清流

9 Ancient Coin

What the hell is that stuff
rotten cords are shameful
an empty purse still holds something
the ages value honesty

The third-century official Wang Yan was known for his vanity
and pretentious use of language. He was so careful to avoid
the appearance of corruption that he refused to use the word
money and called it "that stuff" instead. Song prefaces Wang's
colloquial usage with one of his own. Until the beginning
of the twentieth century, most Chinese coins had a hole in
the middle that allowed them to be strung together to form
larger denominations. "Rotten cords" suggests unused coins,
hence excessive wealth.

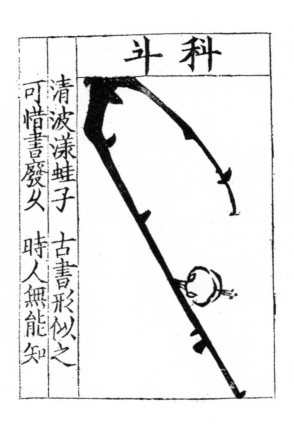

科斗

清波漾蛙子　古書形似之

可惜書廢久　時人無能知

20 Tadpole

A polliwog in crystal water
ancient writing looked like this
out of use so long alas
people now don't know its meaning

Among the earliest means of writing used by the Chinese
was a bamboo stylus they dipped in black lacquer. In con-
trast to the more angular characters carved on metal and
bone during the same period, these early written forms
consisted of black drops and squiggly lines and continue to
require considerable effort to decipher whenever they come
to light. Song wonders what else people of his day no longer
understand.

蝸角

蠻觸國誰雄　戰爭猶未息

由此奪虛名　費盡人間力

31 Snail Horns

Which is stronger Man or Chu
locked in endless warfare
fighting over empty names
squandering their people's strength

Zhuangzi once used the example of a snail to urge rulers to shun the counsel of war. The horns of a snail, he said, were actually two countries named Man and Chu (names meaning "Rude" and "Offensive") that were engaged in an endless cycle of warfare over control of the empty space that stretched between them (*Zhuangzi* 25.4). Song uses his metaphor here to comment on the conflict between the Jurchen-controlled Northern Song and the Chinese-controlled Southern Song dynasties.

歌器

溢滿而覆虛　盈虧俱有病

萬事得于中　烏乎云不正

39 Tilting Bowl

Fill it and it empties
too little or too much are faults
all things have their balance
don't think this one isn't right

This "bowl-on-a-swivel" was placed next to the throne to remind the emperor that shortage and excess both lead to disaster. Only when the bowl was half-full was it stable. According to Xunzi, Confucius saw a device like this in the ancestral hall of Duke Huan: "An attendant poured water into a container that hung at an angle. As the water level approached the midpoint, the container became upright. But when the attendant went beyond the midpoint, it tipped over, the water poured out, and it hung empty once more. Seeing this, Confucius sighed, 'Alas! Whatever becomes full becomes empty.'" (*Xunzi* 28)

颦眉

西施無限愁　後人何必傚
只好笑呵呵　不損紅粧貌

49 Pinched Eyebrows

Why must others imitate
Xi Shi's constant frown
better just to giggle
it won't ruin your rouge

Xi Shi was one of the most famous beauties of ancient China. In the fifth century BCE, the king of Yue presented her to his nemesis, the king of Wu, hoping she would distract him from attending to government affairs, an assignment in which she succeeded, much to the king of Wu's regret. Among her famous attributes were pinched eyebrows, reportedly caused by a heart condition. When other women heard how beautiful she was, they tried to copy her frown but only succeeded in making themselves look foolish.

開鏡

爛熳二十八枝

塵匣啓菱花
醜妍無不識
羞殺幾英雄
霜鬢太煎逼

51 Opening the Mirror

Lifting the *ling* flower from its case
thereby revealing the lovely and ugly
frightening how many heroes
with a sudden attack of white hair

Bronze mirrors entered China via the Silk Road as early as 4,000 years ago and remained the primary means of reflection until the eighteenth century, when they were finally replaced by those of silvered glass. These early bronze mirrors were rarely bigger than a person's hand but were sufficiently convex to reflect the whole face. The back was covered with symbols and designs and included a protruding boss in the middle with a hole through which a cord was attached that allowed the mirror to be picked up from its protective box without getting fingerprints on the polished side. Most mirrors were round, but a popular shape during the Tang and Song dynasties was the eight-petaled *ling,* or water caltrop, flower. It was meant to remind those who used it of the purity of water and of water's ability to reflect their true appearance.

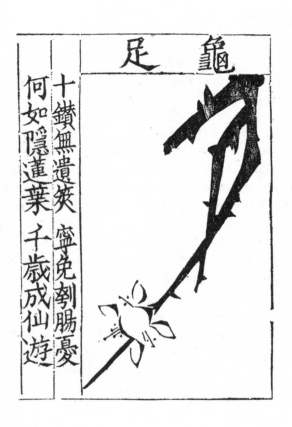

龜足

十鑽無遺筴　寧免剚腸憂
何如隱蓮葉　千歲成仙遊

63 Turtle Feet

A shell full of holes
or freedom from knives
better to vanish beneath lily pads
to be a wandering immortal for a thousand years

Turtles were thought to live thousands of years and to possess knowledge of the future. To access this knowledge, the Chinese drilled and heated their upper shell and lower plastron and interpreted the resulting cracks to predict coming events. Once, when Zhuangzi was fishing along the Pu River, two emissaries from the state of Chu approached him and said, "Our lord wishes to entrust administration of his realm to you." Without bothering to put down his pole, Zhuangzi replied, "I've heard that your king has a 3,000-year-old turtle shell he keeps on his ancestral altar. Do you think the turtle would rather be dead and have its shell so honored or be alive and dragging its tail in the mud? Leave me be. I would rather drag my tail in the mud." (*Zhuangzi* 17.11)

漉酒巾

爛醉是生涯　折腰良可恥
欲酒對黃華　烏紗奚足愛

80 Wine-Straining Bandanna

Falling down drunk is the life for me
bowing at the waist is so depressing
I'd rather face chrysanthemums with wine
a black silk hat isn't worth my time

The character for chrysanthemum 菊 is a homophone for the character for old age 久. Both were pronounced *kiu* when this was written. With that in mind, the Chinese infused its yellow petals in alcohol to celebrate longevity in the fall. It was the favorite flower of the early fifth-century poet Tao Yuanming, who was known for his love of chrysanthemums and rice wine as well as for his disdain of official position. Chinese officials and members of the gentry were rarely without some sort of head covering. A hat of black silk was customary for officials carrying out their normal duties, while a simple bandanna was worn by peasants or people of modest means. Tao Yuanming was known to take his off to strain wine, then to wring it out and put it back on his head.

歌風

暗香從何來　寒颸爲輕扇
東君須護持　莫點宮粧面

90 Windblown

Where does that hidden scent come from
wafted by a winter gale
may the Lord of the East protect it
and keep it from gracing palace faces

The phrase "hidden scent" is another name for the plum
blossom and recalls Lin Bu's famous poem "Small Plum
Tree in a Mountain Garden" (see *Poems of the Masters* 220).
The Lord of the East refers to the sun, the ruler of spring,
at whose impending approach the plum surprises the win-
ter landscape with its blossoms. In addition to powder and
paint, palace ladies also decorated their faces with moistened
petals, a custom some say began with Yang Guifei, the con-
sort of Emperor Xuanzong.

獨 釣

一竿風雨寒　　獨占嚴陵瀨

苟非伸腳眠　　曷見光武大

98 Fishing Alone

Living apart at Yanling Bend
his pole in the cold windblown rain
sleeping with his feet stretched out
he showed us Guangwu's stature

Yan Ziling lived in the first century and spent his days fishing
from a rock along an especially scenic stretch of the Fuchun
River south of Hangzhou. He was once visited there by
his boyhood companion who had since restored the Han
dynasty and ascended the throne as Emperor Guangwu (see
poem 1). Unimpressed with his friend's attainments, Yan
stretched out and fell asleep with his feet on the emperor's
stomach. The incident did much to immortalize Guangwu
as a tolerant ruler. No doubt, Song Boren is hoping for the
same treatment from his.

POEMS OF THE MASTERS

Poems of the Masters 千家詩

When I was first living in Taiwan in the 1970s, I tried my hand at a number of arts, none of them with any success. One of my failures was calligraphy. A Chinese friend arranged for me to study with Zhuang Yan 莊嚴, the curator of the Palace Museum's painting and calligraphy collection. I was both honored and embarrassed to have such a teacher, and I tried. Every Saturday afternoon I visited him at his home next to the museum and showed him what I had done during the week. He was always encouraging. But it was hopeless.

One Saturday after my lesson, I told him I had heard that the Chinese don't read poetry the way we do in the West, that they intone or sing poems. He said that was true. I asked him, if that was so, how do readers know how to do it: There are no notations on the page. He said, "Just a minute," and went into another room. When he came back out, he put a bottle of Taiwan whiskey on the table. "That," he said, "is how we sing them. It's up to you."

I couldn't help smiling at the thought of inebriation being viewed as an essential part of reading—and I assumed composing—poetry. I loved the prospect, but I couldn't help wondering where such a view came from. No one I asked had an answer. After six months of failure, I finally gave up on calligraphy, but I didn't give up on finding out why the Chinese sang their poems, even if they might not have a bottle of whiskey within reach.

The answer came to me a few months later while I was working my way through China's first poetry anthology, the *Shijing* 詩經, or *Book of Poetry*. It was compiled by Confucius around 500 BCE, and my edition included a preface written by the second-century erudite Zheng Xuan 鄭玄, in which he presented China's first definition of poetry—a definition still quoted today by Chinese poets and by those who read poetry. Zheng wrote: "In the heart, it's what a person holds dear. Expressed in language, it's poetry." "Words from the heart," I said to myself. And we all know what a little whiskey can do in helping open that inner square-inch of ours.

Unfortunately, I had a hard time reconciling Zheng's definition with the poems in the anthology. The poems in the *Shijing* dated back centuries before Confucius's time, and the language seemed so staid. Apparently, Confucius intended his selection for diplomats, so that they could recite something familiar to the members of the courts they visited. I tried, but I simply couldn't intone the collection's four-syllable lines without making them sound like jingles.

I moved on to China's next poetry anthology. Sometime around 200–150 BCE, someone put together a collection called the *Chuci* 楚辭, or *Songs of Chu*. Unlike the *Shijing*, the *Chuci* contained works by known individuals, and they weren't from the Yellow River watershed, from which Confucius collected his poems, but from the southern state of Chu that straddled both sides of the Yangzi. The voices were also different—often verging on the ecstatic, which isn't surprising, as many of the poets were shamans. The poetics, too, were different. The lines were longer and more varied, ranging from six to eight syllables, and they were easy to sing. I had no trouble imagining Zhuang Yan's bottle on my table. The problem, though, was that they weren't easy to understand. I had been spoiled by Cold Mountain and Stonehouse, who wrote to be understood.

I wasn't alone. Although these two anthologies formed an essential part of the education of the elite in the distant past, few people read them today other than students of Chinese literature. The ancient poems most people still read are from a different era, namely, the Tang (618–906) and Song (960–1278) dynasties. This was considered the Golden Age of Chinese poetry. And there was a reason it came to be called that. In the seventh century the court decided to make examinations in poetry and prose the basis of their civil service. The literary arts soon became the doors to advancement. These arts had been developing in China for millennia, but in the Tang and Song they became the coins of the realm and as common as filtered rice wine—not universal but certainly within the reach of millions more people than before.

What aroused my interest was that near the end of this Golden Age its highlights were summarized in another, more accessible, anthology: the *Qianjiashi*, or *Poems of the Masters*. This collection was compiled by Liu Kezhuang 劉克莊 at the very end of the Song. Liu was one of the leading literary critics of that dynasty, and he decided to present his views on poetry through a collection of examples. Although no copy of Liu's original anthology survives, it was a great success, as it enjoyed the good fortune of being published at the beginning of China's printing revolution. It soon appeared not just in private academies but also in village schools across the country, where it established itself as eminently useful in teaching students the rhythms of language and of the heart, as well as the names of all sorts of things.

Over the centuries, Liu's anthology was expanded from 200 to the present 224 poems. Also, instead of the poems being arranged according to subject matter, they were re-arranged according to poetic form, depending on the number of characters, or syllables, in a line and whether the rhyme scheme and tonal pattern followed the rules laid down for *jueju* 絕句 (detached quatrains) or *lushi* 律詩 (regulated verse).

What distinguished *Poems of the Masters* from all previous anthologies was that it made poetry accessible to everyone. In fact, some commentators have preferred to read the title to mean: *Poems for the Thousands*. Until the Cultural Revolution, it was part of every student's education, beginning as early as the third grade. The reason for this was its inclusion of poems everyone could understand and appreciate. Finally, something I could not only sing but also understand. While the poems of the *Shijing* and the *Chuci* are certainly worth reading, anyone who wants to understand what the Chinese hold dear couldn't do better than to read the poems of the heart they know by heart. The whiskey is up to you.

from *Poems of the Masters*

1 Spring Dawn

Sleeping in spring oblivious of dawn
in every direction I hear birds
after the wind and rain last night
I wonder how many petals fell

2 Calling on Censor Yuan without Success

In Luoyang I tried to visit you sir
but to Jiangling you were banished
the plum I hear flowers earlier there
but how could spring compare

---

[1] By Meng Haoran 孟浩然 (d. 740). Meng was one of the few poets who didn't pursue an official career. He spent most of his life in his hometown of Xiangyang or at his hermitage on nearby Lumenshan.

[2] Another poem by Meng. Luoyang was three hundred kilometers north of Meng's home. Failing to meet an official to whom he had written, he commiserates. Jiangling was on the Yangzi, and the seasons were different. Obviously, his friend wouldn't be spending the new year at home.

5 Sitting Alone on Jingting Mountain

Flocks of birds disappear in the distance
lone clouds wander away
who never tires of my company
only Jingting Mountain

6 Climbing White Crane Tower

The midday sun slips behind the mountains
the Yellow River turns for the sea
trying to see for a thousand miles
I climb one more story

[5] By Li Bai 李白 (d. 762). For a brief period, Li Bai was a favorite of the court. But he soon fell into disfavor and spent the rest of his life wandering along the Yangzi, a guest of those who appreciated his talent and spirit. He wrote this in 753 in Xuancheng. This mountain was just north of the city wall.

[6] By Wang Zhihuan 王之渙 (d. 742). Wang failed to pass the official exams and spent his days visiting friends and scenic spots in his home province of Shanxi. This three-story tower was located at the southern end of the province in the town of Yongji, where the Yellow River comes down from the north and turns east on the other side of the Zhongtiao Mountains.

15 Ballad of Changgan

Where are you from good sir
this maid is from Hengtang
I ask while our boats are moored
perhaps we're from the same place

21 Ode to the Autumn Wind

Where does the autumn wind come from
rising it sees off the geese
entering the courtyard trees at dawn
it wakes a lone traveler first

[15] By Cui Hao 崔顥 (d. 754). Cui was greatly admired by Li Bai and like him did not enjoy a successful career. Hengtang was the name of the embankment along the Jinhuai River where it flowed past Nanjing into the nearby Yangzi. Where the two rivers met was called Changgan.

[21] A poem by Liu Yuxi 劉禹錫 (d. 842). Although Liu held several important posts, he was repeatedly demoted because of poems he wrote satirizing those in power. The autumn wind reminds him of the end of the summer of his life and the loss of imperial favor. Like the geese, he is headed south, away from the capital, from which he has been banished.

26   Looking for a Recluse without Success

Below the pines I ask a boy
he says his master has gone to find herbs
he's somewhere on this mountain
but the clouds are too thick to know where

29   Thoughts on a Quiet Night

Before my bed the light is so bright
it looks like a layer of frost
lifting my head I gaze at the moon
lying back down I think of home

[26] By Jia Dao 賈島 (d. 843). Jia Dao became a Buddhist monk when he was young but later changed his mind and decided to return to lay life so he could devote himself to poetry. This poem is set in the Zhongnan Mountains south of Chang'an.

[29] Another poem by Li Bai. This is one of his most famous. Critics sigh at the effortlessness of his technique and ability to transport the reader not only to a place but to a state of mind. When the Chinese see the moon, it reminds them that friends and family elsewhere are looking at it too.

39 In Reply

Somehow I ended up beneath pines
sleeping in comfort on boulders
there aren't any calendars in the mountains
winter ends but who counts the years

52 The Zhongnan Mountains

Taiyi isn't far from the Heart of Heaven
its ridges extend to the edge of the sea
white clouds form before one's eyes
blue vapors vanish in plain sight
around its peaks the whole realm turns
in every valley the light looks different
needing a place to spend the night
I yelled to a woodcutter across the stream

[39] Nothing is known about the author of this poem, other than that he lived in the Zhongnan Mountains south of Chang'an and called himself the Ancient Recluse 太上隱者.

[52] By Wang Wei 王維 (d. 761). Wandering in his favorite mountains south of the capital, Wang finds himself too far from his country estate to return by dusk. Taiyi (the Great One) was the range's highest peak. "The Heart of Heaven" refers to a Daoist paradise.

60   To Zhang Xu after Drinking

The world is full of fickle people
you old friend aren't one
inspired you write like a god
drunk you're crazier still
enjoying white hair and idle days
suddenly blue clouds rise before you
how many more times will you sleep
with a jug of wine by your bed

63   Recording My Thoughts While Traveling at Night

A shore of thin reeds in light wind
a tall boat alone at night
stars hang over a barren land
the moon rises out of the Yangzi
how could writing ever lead to fame
I quit my post due to illness and age
drifting along what am I like
a solitary gull between Heaven and Earth

---

[60] By Gao Shi 高適 (d. 765). This is about a friend whose cursive script became more inspired as he drank. "Blue clouds" refers to high position. Alas, his friend's new post will require earlier hours.

[63] By Du Fu 杜甫 (d. 770). He wrote this after the death of his patron in Chengdu, as he sailed down the Yangzi looking for a new refuge. A tall boat is one with a sail.

72/73 Encountering Rain at Zhangba Reservoir Late One Afternoon While Enjoying a Cool Breeze with Rich Young Men and Their Singsong Girls—Two Poems

Sunset is just right for boating
a light breeze stirs a few waves
boaters pause by the dense bamboo
enjoying the cool lotus-flower air
the young men add ice to their drinks
the women scrape lotus roots clean
a cloud overhead turns dark
surely the rain will bring poems

Rain soaks through the canopy mats
wind beats against the prow
girls from Yue wring out their red skirts
girls from Yan lament their mascara
even with the boat tied to a willow
the awning still lifts in the spray
the road home looks desolate now
on a fall day in May at the lake

[72] Poems by Du Fu about an outing at the reservoir that supplied water to the capital. Ice was stored underground in straw-filled boxes and sold in summer to those who could afford it.

[73] The ancient states of Yue and Yan were known for their female entertainers.

77 Passing Xiangji Temple

Oblivious of Xiangji Temple
I walked through mountains of clouds
ancient trees a deserted path
somewhere in the hills a bell
the sound of the stream choking on boulders
sunlight on the cold green pines
by a silent pool in fading light
meditation tamed the serpent

85 Casual Poem on a Spring Day

Clouds are thin the wind is light the sun is nearly overhead
past the flowers through the willows down along the stream
people don't see the joy in my heart
they think I'm wasting time or acting like a child

[77] Another poem by Wang Wei. Xiangji Temple was on a plateau fifteen kilometers southwest of Chang'an. It was the earliest seat of Pure Land Buddhism in China. Wang Wei was a student of Zen, in which meditation is coupled with wisdom. The serpent is a reference to desire.

[85] By Cheng Hao 程顥 (d. 1085). Together with his younger brother, Cheng Yi, Cheng Hao was one of the major advocates of the Neo-Confucian revival that dominated intellectual life in the Song. During the ten years he taught in Luoyang, his students numbered in the thousands.

88 Early Spring East of Town

The best time for a poet is when spring is new
when willows turn gold but not completely
if you wait until the Royal Woods look like brocade
the whole town will be out gawking at flowers

90 Light Rain in Early Spring

The streets of Heaven glisten from light rain
grass appears far off but not nearby
this is truly the best time of spring
when the sight of misty willows fills the royal city

[88] By Yang Juyuan 楊巨源 (d. 834). Yang rose to become director of studies at the imperial university. The Chinese love to look for the first signs of spring. The Royal Woods consisted of groves of pear and chestnut trees planted adjacent to the palace in Chang'an.

[90] By Han Yu 韓愈 (d. 824). Han Yu was one of the most famous literary figures of the Tang and its most ardent supporter of Confucian ideals. Here, the angle of view from his home on the plateau south of the capital condenses the faint colors on the horizon, whereby green appears in the distance but not nearby, and the myriad new willow catkins look like so much mist.

109 Visiting a Private Garden without Success

It must be because he hates clogs on his moss
I knocked ten times still his gate stayed closed
but spring can't be kept locked inside a garden
a branch of red blossoms reached past the wall

114 The Peach Blossoms of Xuandu Temple

The purple path's red dust swirling before their faces
everyone says *we've been to see the flowers*
a thousand peach trees at Xuandu Temple
all of them planted since Mister Liu departed

[109] By Ye Shaoweng 葉紹翁 (fl. 1200–1250). Little else is known about Ye,
other than that he served as an academician. These clogs are still worn
in Japan at home and at public baths, but no longer in China. They had
two wooden ridges on the bottom. The one in front helped when going
uphill, and the one in back when going downhill. The red blossoms are
most likely those of the apricot.

[114] This and the next poem are by Liu Yuxi. Liu wrote this one in 815 upon
returning to Chang'an after a ten-year banishment for siding with the
reform faction. The combination of allusions resulted in a second banish-
ment. This Daoist temple was located three kilometers from the capital's
South Gate. "Red dust" refers to the material world, and "the purple path"
to the royal thoroughfare of Red Bird Street, along which the wealthy and
well-connected lived.

115   Visiting Xuandu Temple Again

The temple's vast courtyard is now home to moss
vegetables are flowering where peach trees once bloomed
where is the priest who planted the trees
Old Mister Liu is back here again

117   Flower Shadows

Layer upon layer on the alabaster terrace
I tell the boy to sweep them up in vain
just as the sun takes them all away
the full moon brings them back again

[115] Upon returning to Chang'an in 828, Liu wrote, "I am back again, this time to serve as director of the Bureau of Receptions. Once more, I visited Xuandu Temple, but not a single tree was standing—nothing but weeds swayed in the spring breeze. Thus, I am writing four more lines in anticipation of my next visit." Not long after writing this poem, he was banished yet again.

[117] By Su Shi 蘇軾 (d. 1101). Famous not only for his poetry and calligraphy, Su was also one of the most prominent political figures of the Song dynasty. This is read by some as a political critique: with the alabaster terrace representing the Song court, the flowers the reforms of Wang Anshi, the sun the empress dowager, who canceled the reforms, the moon her son—the new emperor—who reintroduced them, and the shadows their perceived benefits. Symbolism aside, the poem does fine without such baggage.

126 Events of Late Spring

House swallows swoop above my desk in pairs
willow fuzz floats in my inkwell
sitting below my window reading the *Book of Changes*
I wonder how long spring has been over

127 Climbing a Hill

All day I felt lost as if drunk or in a dream
hearing spring was over I decided to climb a hill
beyond my bamboo garden I met a monk and talked
and spent another afternoon beyond this floating life

[126] By Ye Cai 葉采 (c. 1190–1240). A famous Confucian scholar of his day and director of the Palace Library in Hangzhou, Ye makes fun of his own immersion in the philosophy of change and his failure to pay attention to the changes taking place around him. The *Book of Changes* was the primary text used by Neo-Confucians during the Song dynasty for developing something comparable to Daoist cosmology and Buddhist psychology.

[127] By Li She 李涉 (fl. 830). Preferring the simpler, unfettered life into which he was born, Li and his younger brother lived as recluses. Later, he was recommended to the court and served briefly as an adviser to the crown prince. Because he did not get along with those in power, he was "rusticated," much to his delight.

128 Lament of the Silk Maid

During the fourth watch the cuckoo cries
she gets up to check if the silkworms have enough leaves
surprised at the moon between the rooftops and willows
and her mistress not back from the party

131 Seeing Off Spring

In April fading flowers fall but more appear
back and forth swallows fly all day below the eaves
the cuckoo cries at midnight as if its voice would break
not convinced it can't call the East Wind back

[128] By Xie Fangde 謝枋得 (d. 1289). Xie served in several posts in the Hang-zhou area, which is still famous for its silk brocade. During this period, taxes were paid in lengths of silk, and each household had a quota to meet and someone assigned to fill it, which required a massive amount of mulberry leaves. The cuckoo's call is said to sound like the phrase *bu-ru gui-qu* 不如歸去, "better go home." The night was divided into five two-hour watches.

[131] By Wang Fengyuan 王逢原 (d. 1059). Wang was quite poor, but he came to the attention of the prime minister, Wang Anshi, and had a promising future. Unfortunately, he died before he was thirty. The swallow is the bird most commonly associated with summer, while the oriole and cuckoo are the birds of early and late spring, respectively. The East Wind is the wind of spring and the West Wind the wind of autumn.

132 Seeing Off Spring on the Last Day of April

When you finally reach the last day of April
your wind and light forsake a poor poet
I don't need to sleep with you tonight
until the dawn bell you're still spring

135 Waking Up in Early Summer

The sour trace of plums squirts between my teeth
the light green of banana leaves fills my window screen
waking up at noon without a thought or care
I sit and watch my children chasing willow fuzz

[132] Another poem by Jia Dao. A former monk, Jia Dao failed to attain even minor distinction as an official but became well known for his plaintive, well-crafted verses, some of which took years to write. The bell is that of a monastery, which will soon be rousing his former colleagues trying to transcend their attachments.

[135] By Yang Wanli 楊萬里 (d. 1206). When he was serving as an official, Yang experienced an enlightenment he equated with that of Zen and began writing in a simple, spontaneous style. Here, he wakes from a midday nap and watches his children chase willow fuzz, which is itself a sign that spring is over. Such are the pleasures of early summer for those who don't chase fame or fortune.

137   Impressions

Swaying bamboo shadows shroud my secluded window
summer birds chatter in pairs in the sunset
begonias have faded and willow fuzz has flown
the enervating days are starting to get longer

139   Written at the South Tower of Ezhou

Mountain light meets water light everywhere I look
from the railing I can smell miles of water lilies
the soft wind and bright moon no one controls
together from the south bring us something cool

[137] By Zhu Shuzhen 朱淑貞 (fl. 1200). Zhu was one of China's most famous woman poets and lived near (and later, in) Hangzhou, which was known for its hot, humid summers. Houses of the rich included inner courtyards, hidden from the view of visitors. The birds remind Zhu of her isolation, and the last signs of spring of her own fading beauty.

[139] By Huang Tingjian 黃庭堅 (d. 1105). Huang was one of the great calligraphers and poets of the Song and also the founder of the Jiangxi school of poetics known for its layered allusions and irregular rhythms. He wrote this on his way into banishment when he stopped at Ezhou's lily-covered South Lake. The South Wind was a common metaphor for benevolent government.

141 Farm Family

Weeding fields at sunup twisting hemp at night
village boys and girls all have their chores
even little children too small to plow or weave
learn to plant melons in the shade of mulberry trees

143 On the Pomegranate Flower

Pomegranate flowers brighten eyes in June
as soon as they appear their fruit begins to form
but neither carts nor horses visit this poor place
where ruby blossoms lie upon the emerald moss

[141] By Fan Chengda 范成大 (d. 1193). Fan was ranked as one of the four great poets of the Southern Song and known for his focus on everyday events. This is one of a series of sixty poems he wrote entitled "Occasional Poems on the Four Seasons of Farm Life." The mulberry produced the leaves that fed the silkworms that made the silk that paid the taxes that supported the imperial lifestyle.

[143] By Zhu Xi 朱熹 (d. 1200). Zhu was chiefly known as one of the leading proponents of Neo-Confucianism. The pomegranate arrived from Central Asia and became so popular that people started calling the fifth lunar month, when the fruit first begins to form, Pomegranate Month. The poet is also reminded that, like the pomegranate and its seeds, his own Neo-Confucian ideas are full of promise.

144　Village Dusk

Grass lines the pond and water laps against the bank
the sun sinks in the mountains and in the ripples
a herd boy returns on the back of his ox
aimlessly blowing a flute to no tune

147　Seeing Off Yuan Er on a Mission to Anxi

Morning rain dampens the dust in Weicheng
new willow catkins turn an inn green
drink one more cup of wine my friend
west of Yang Pass there's no one you know

[144] By Lei Chen 雷震. Nothing is known about Lei, which is surprising, as
commentators marvel at the combination of effortlessness and craftsman-
ship in this poem. The transverse flute was invented in prehistoric times
by nomadic groups and first made from eagle bones, which the Chinese
replaced with bamboo.

[147] Another poem by Wang Wei. Here he sees off a friend banished to Anxi,
the westernmost post of Chinese control on the Silk Road. Weicheng was
across the Wei River from Chang'an and was where people held going-
away parties for friends heading west. The Chinese character for "willow"
柳 is a homophone for 留 meaning "stay." Thus, the Chinese broke off
willow catkins to give to friends as a parting memento.

148   On Yellow Crane Tower Hearing a Flute

Suddenly an exile on my way to Changsha
I look west toward Chang'an for my home in vain
on Yellow Crane Tower I hear a jade flute
plum blossoms fall in this city in June

154   Mid-Autumn Moon

As evening clouds withdraw a clear cool air floods in
the jade wheel passes silently across the Silver River
this life this night has rarely been kind
where will we see this moon next year

[148] Another poem by Li Bai. He wrote this one in 758 when he stopped to visit Yellow Crane Tower in Wuchang. He had just been released from prison in nearby Jiujiang for his involvement in the revolt of the emperor's brother and was being banished further south to Changsha. Li was from Chengdu, but he was hoping to make Chang'an his home. "Plum Blossoms Fall" was the name of a tune for the flute. The plum normally blooms during New Year. Li, like most Chinese, identifies with its ability to transcend winter's adversity.

[154] Another poem by Su Shi (aka Dongpo). He wrote this while serving on the Grand Canal, where he was joined by his brother, Su Che. They spent much of their lives apart at different posts. Still, both made every effort to be together for the Mid-Autumn Festival. The jade wheel is the moon, and the Silver River is the Milky Way.

166   Cold Spring Pavilion

A stream of pure water can soothe a poet's soul
it alone knows how cold the years have been
flowing into West Lake it carries entertainers
looking back it's changed since the mountains

168   Anchored Overnight at Maple Bridge

Crows caw the moon sets and frost fills the sky
river maples fishing fires and care-troubled sleep
from Cold Mountain Temple outside the Suzhou wall
the sound of the midnight bell reaches a traveler's boat

[166] A poem by Lin Zhen 林楨 (fl. 1180) about whom we know nothing. This pavilion was in Hangzhou next to a spring that emptied into West Lake, which became the scene of constant parties following the court's relocation there in 1129.

[168] A poem by Zhang Ji 張繼 (fl. 760). Zhang was traveling along the Grand Canal and moored for the night in the western suburbs of Suzhou. The bridge is still there, a few hundred meters north of Cold Mountain Temple, named for a nearby hill, not the poet. In Suzhou, temple bells were rung at midnight to signify impermanence. Fishermen used torches at night to attract fish and cormorants to catch them.

175 Herd Boy

Across the countryside the grass extends for miles
he blows a few notes on the evening wind
returning home and eating long after sunset
he lies down in the moonlight still wearing his raincoat

178 Written on a Wall

A pile of dry rushes in total disarray
suddenly lights the sky and suddenly is gone
no match for a stove full of old stump wood
slowly steadily giving off heat

175 By Lu Dongbin 呂洞賓 (d. 1016). Lu was the leader of Daoism's Eight Immortals. This poem was also attributed to a herd boy by a Song-dynasty official named Zhong Ruoweng 鍾弱翁.

178 An anonymous poem. Commentators suggest this poem was included as a commentary about goings-on at the Song court.

199   River Village

A clear stream encircles the whole village
in the middle of summer life here is quiet
swallows come and go above the rafters
seagulls meet and mate on the current
my wife draws a chessboard on paper
my children bend needles into fishhooks
as long as friends keep sharing their salary rice
what more does this poor body need

220   Small Plum Tree in a Mountain Garden

When others are gone this flower alone shines forth
usurping entirely my little garden scene
its thin reflection slanting across a pristine pond
its hidden scent floating below the moon at dusk
winter birds look again before they land
butterflies would faint if they but knew
thankfully singing softly I can draw near
I don't need a sounding board or cup of wine

[199] Du Fu wrote this poem in 760 at his cottage in Chengdu. A rebuilt cottage still marks the spot. His friend Bei Di shared part of his salary, which was paid in rice.

[220] By Lin Bu 林逋 (d. 1028). A hermit poet, Lin lived on an island in Hangzhou's West Lake on which he planted hundreds of plum trees, one of which is in bloom in this poem. Poets sometimes tapped on a board when intoning poetry. Wine was optional.

WEI YINGWU

WEI YINGWU 韋應物

During the twenty years I lived in Taiwan (1972–1991), I never lived in the big city of Taipei. Mountain monasteries and farmhouses were such a better option. But sooner or later, I had to go down the mountain. Whenever I did, I invariably included Chongqing South Road on my itinerary. It was only a couple blocks from the train station and was the city's bookstore street. One of my favorites was the store operated by Chunghwa Press 中華書局. They specialized in small five-by-seven hardback reprints of old woodblock editions, which they bound in green cloth. Their books were a pleasure just to hold. One day I picked up one that included the poems of Wei Yingwu, and I couldn't put it down. I took it back to the converted farm shed I was renting on Seven Star Mountain 七星山 and thought I would translate a few. But whenever I found one I thought I understood, I had to put it back on the shelf and work on something easier. The book followed me back to America, but it remained on the shelf. Finally, thirty years after I brought Wei Yingwu home, I decided it was time to get serious about our relationship. What prompted me to make the commitment were two newly published commentaries I found on bookstore street during a return visit to Taiwan.

Readers who don't know Chinese don't realize that knowing Chinese doesn't mean you can understand a poem written a thousand years ago. Even educated Chinese aren't likely to understand one they've never read before. That's why commentaries are so important. For those who wrote to be understood, like Puming or Cold Mountain or Stonehouse, commentaries weren't necessary. But with Wei Yingwu, I could never have proceeded without their help.

It also helps to have the intercession of the gods. In Wei's case, the only biographies were mere sketches. But when I was still working on the poems and happened to travel to China in the fall of 2008, I thought I would look for something more. And so I contacted a scholar I had met in Xi'an. She wasn't able to help, but she passed me on to another scholar who passed me on to another scholar who directed me to an exhibition of tombstones at the Forest of Steles.

Incredibly, on display were those of Wei, his wife, his son, and his son's wife. The four tombstones had only come to light the previous year, when a pair of grave robbers unearthed them in the Wei family cemetery—the location of which remains unknown—and sold them to Gao Ping, a scholar who happened to live near where they were found. Once word got out about the find, officials at the Forest of Steles ordered police to confiscate them and had Gao fired from his post at Northwest University for being in possession of national treasures. Unfortunately, I couldn't get close enough to take photos that were clear, and I was told the museum had not published copies.

Having nothing better to do, the next morning I hired a taxi and drove to Xingjiao Monastery. It was on the Duling Plateau, where the Wei family estate was once located—and where I had searched before without success. As we drove into the monastery parking lot, a layman I had met during one such unsuccessful excursion came running out of the monastery bookstore. He said he had some new information and would call me later. I didn't hear from him, but that night Professor Gao came to my hotel room. He didn't have any information about the location of the Wei family grave, but he gave me digital copies of the epitaphs, along with a transcription of Wei Yingwu's, which was quite helpful, as the facsimile was hard to read in places. It was one of those happy karmic events. Suddenly I could see Wei's life behind the poems. And the more I saw, the more I understood why I liked his poems so much.

Wei Yingwu was born in 737 into one of the most prestigious clans in all of China. But things at court were always changing. By the time he was born, the fortunes of his branch of the clan were on the wane. Still, he was a Wei. When he was fifteen, he was invited to join the palace guard of Emperor Xuanzong. The emperor and his concubine, Yang Guifei, lived as if the gods were their servants. Wei later admitted he was guilty of his own excesses. Then it all ended.

In the winter of 755, An Lushan rebelled and led his army to Chang'an. The emperor fled, and the rebels sacked the city. When imperial forces retook the capital two years later, and the emperor returned, Wei resolved to change his ways. He married and began his career as an official. Being a member of the aristocracy, he was able to bypass the civil service exams and secure minor posts, first in Luoyang, then in Chang'an. It was a good beginning, but it didn't last long. When the patron who arranged such posts was accused of wrongdoing and later executed, the bureaucrats at court treated Wei as an outsider and sent him to the provinces to serve along the Yangzi, far from his friends and family.

Wei's final post was as magistrate of Suzhou, where he died in 791. Bai Juyi became magistrate of the same city in 824. Bai was the most famous poet of his day and wrote, "Wei of Suzhou leaves me speechless, the feeling in his poems is so pure and serene." Bai liked Wei's poems so much, he had them carved in stone. He wasn't alone in his admiration, but it wasn't until the Song dynasty that Wei was finally recognized as one of the great poets of the Tang.

The reason Wei remained relatively unknown for so long was that the bureaucrats, who doubled as literary critics, treated him with disdain—not that Wei cared. His hero was the fifth-century poet Tao Yuanming, who quit his post and spent the rest of his life as a farmer. Wei toyed with the idea of following Tao's example, and actually did for a few years, but his sense of responsibility was too great. His fellow officials mouthed the teachings of Confucius. Wei lived them, or tried to. Also, by his own admission, he didn't do well in a crowd. He preferred the company of one or two others, those with whom he didn't have to put on airs and with whom he could share his heart. That is what drew me to his poems. They were meant for friends.

from *In Such Hard Times*

1   The Ninth

On this day of drink and depression
I think about life on our Duling farm
where will I be on the Ninth next year
in such hard times I can't hope to go home

5   Waiting for Lu Hao, Who Writes Saying
He Can't Come Because the Day Is Late and He Has
No Horse, I Send This Poem in Reply

Such a fine day shouldn't be missed
I hoped you would finally honor my door
South Street is still full of people
and West Grove isn't dark yet
I lean on my staff by the gate in vain
your cup waits alone in the garden
don't say you lack a conveyance
I know you have an old cart

[1] Written in the fall of 756 at Fufeng, where Wei took refuge after the sack of Chang'an in 755. Nine is the ultimate *yang* number. On Double Ninth men congratulate themselves on having lived as long as they have.

[5] Written in 765 in Luoyang. South Street ran between the palace of the eastern capital and across the Luo River to the southern part of the city. West Grove was a park along the north bank next to the palace walls.

7   Entertaining Adjutant Li

When we were fifteen we both served at court
we climbed the red steps through incense at dawn
toured the Han Garden in bloom
and bathed on Lishan in the snow
but the Immortal has flown and isn't expected back
his advisers are scattered assuming they're alive
meeting you today thinking about the past
one cup makes me happy the next one sad

28   On My Day Off Visiting Censor Wang and Finding Him Gone

Nine days of being busy then a day of rest
I didn't find you home and came back disappointed
no wonder your poems chill a person's bones
your door faces an icy stream and snow-covered hills

[7] Written in 765 in Luoyang. Wei became a member of the imperial guard when he was fifteen. The royal garden was laid out earlier in the Han dynasty along the Qujiang Canal and was the Tang court's favorite resort in spring. The hot springs of Lishan were thirty kilometers east of Chang'an and were where Emperor Xuanzong and his concubine Yang Guifei spent winters. Xuanzong died in 762 and is referred to euphemistically.

[28] Written in 772 in Luoyang. Officials had one day off every ten days. A censor was in charge of reporting government, even imperial, abuses.

38   Describing My Feelings to Commandant Lu

The straight and the square rarely advance
I'm serving in the stupidest of posts
I don't have time to open a book
buried beneath casework and records
the disaster of war has worn us all down
there's no vacation from corvée and taxes
the downtrodden masses need help
but compassionate measures cause trouble
I think of retiring day and night
from outside my door I can see the old mountains
if you're feeling the same as me
let's go home arm-in-arm together

43   Jade Diggers Ballad

The government drafts a common man
tells him to dig for Lan River jade
over the ridge nights away from home
he sleeps in thickets of thorns in the rain
his wife returns from taking him food
she sobs looking south from their home

[38] Written in 775 in Chang'an. The government conscripted one able-bodied male from every family for public works projects. Wei was in charge of work gangs in the capital area.

[43] Written in the fall of 775 on a mission to Lantian, famous for its jade.

51   On a Mission to Yunyang: To the Prefecture Staff

I left at dawn on the magistrate's orders
to brave flames and not to dally
a hundred *li* later I reached Yunyang
at every village I asked about flooding
the forces of Heaven keep going astray
why aren't its blessings bestowed fairly
looking at the tops of tall trees
I could see the traces of disaster
perfectly good crops in the river
creepers growing back so soon
ancient towns filled with rubble
once happy homes in ruins
I waded down flooded roads on my tour
whole hillsides were washed away
our wise and kind magistrate was concerned for the people
I myself volunteered for this duty
meanwhile you gentlemen at court
gossip and laugh and think about parties

[51] Written in the summer of 777 on a mission to survey flood damage north
of Chang'an. In his capacity in the Labor Bureau, Wei would have been
charged with rebuilding the roads and bridges—hence his visit. He must
have annoyed others with his assessment of their concern, but the magis-
trate of Chang'an, Li Huan, was his patron. Still, such an attitude betrays
the aloofness of an aristocrat who can't conceal his disdain for bureaucrats
committed to no other ideal than their own welfare.

52   Lamenting My Loss

Like white silk that has been dyed
or wood that is now ashes
I recall the person I lived with
gone and not returning
to whom I was wedded for twenty years
who respected me as if we just met
our betrothal occurred during troubled times
our separations were due to disasters
a model of gentleness and simplicity
she was courteous and always proper
but public office has no room for oneself
and my duties undercut her beauty
this morning when I entered her quarters
the rooms were covered with dust
ever since she departed
whatever I touch is painful
a widower now I pass the time
wiping our children's tears
I try to push my fantasies away
but these feelings are hard to stop
suddenly my daydreams look real
startled I begin pacing again
my heart is utterly relentless
and our house is surrounded by weeds

[52] Written in the fall of 777 in Chang'an following the death of his wife.

55   The Funeral

Suddenly the time is here
the auspicious chosen day
the team of horses whinny
the hearse departs the ancestral hall
this was where we lived our lives
until we were parted by death
what good is this brief moment
if we just end up in the hills
the cortege left by the city's South Gate
southward I gazed toward the ragged ridges
the sun went down and clouds appeared
I cried all night in the bitter wind
into the tomb I looked at dawn
saying farewell I could only tremble
into the ground the coffin vanished
I looked up at the sun's bright light
a moment later it was over
even the graveside trees looked bleak
I stood there unable to move
I couldn't leave with my heart in a knot
our daughter sensed what we had lost
she wailed and clutched my robe
this is still too sudden
and the months and years too hard to forget

[55] Written in the fall of 777 at the family gravesite.

56   Letting My Eyes Roam at Mei Reservoir While Serving as Magistrate of Huxian

White water surges along the embankment
mist swirls in a sunny sky
green is taking over the trees
there's jade on a thousand mountains
fish are swimming up to the surface
lotuses aren't thick yet
I come here to be alone with my thoughts
I regret lacking social skills

57   The Call of the Cuckoo

Dew drips from tall trees on a clear summer night
in the hills to the south a cuckoo calls
the widow next door comforts her child
I turn in bed and wait for first light

[56] Written in the summer of 778 in Huxian. Wei's patron, Li Huan, arranged for this appointment to a town fifty kilometers southwest of Chang'an, providing Wei a place to grieve the loss of his wife. The Mei River flows out of the Zhongnan Mountains and into a reservoir just west of Huxian.

[57] Written in the summer of 778 in Huxian, a year after the death of his wife. The cuckoo is a harbinger of the end of spring, and its plaintive cry is also associated with loss.

60 In Reply to Daoist Master Donglin

How many peaks are you west of Zige
in your hut on a snowy night beside those tiger tracks
if I knew where you were in that distant blackness
I would follow your evening bell all the way past the temple

61 Visiting the Ferry in the Western Suburbs Again

Where the river winds I reflect on my travels
a traveler lost in reminiscence again
the moon last night was so lovely
I've come back to see it in the waves
birds won't roost where they feel afraid
or a fragrance spread where it's cold
when will I hold someone's hand again
the flowers overhead look like sleet

[60] Written in the winter of 778 in Huxian. Zige (Purple Pavilion) was the
name of a peak in the Zhongnan Mountains fifteen kilometers southeast
of Huxian. The South China tiger was a bit bigger than a German shep-
herd. It is now nearly extinct. The trail to Zige Peak went past the famous
Buddhist monastery known as Zige or Baolin Temple.

[61] Written in the spring of 779. This was one of eight poems Wei wrote
about his visits to this area along the Feng River halfway between Huxian
and Chang'an. He retired here the following year.

71 In Imitation of Tao Pengze

When other plants bow to the frost
chrysanthemums alone show their beauty
this is the nature of things
there's no changing the seasons
I sprinkle their petals in homemade wine
at sunset I sit down with farmers
under thatched eaves all of us drunk
life is about more than plenty

73 In Reply to Commissioner Cui

A courtyard of bamboo and late-night snow
a lone lantern a book on the table
if I hadn't encountered the teaching of no effort
how else could I have achieved this life of leisure

[71] Written in the fall of 780 on the Feng River at Shanfu Hermitage, where
he "retired." Tao Pengze is another name for Tao Yuanming, Wei's hero,
who served as an official in Pengze County but found official life tedious
and retired to take up farming. Wei is celebrating the Double Ninth, when
men drink wine infused with chrysanthemum petals.

[73] Written in the winter of 780 at his hermitage. Cui Zhuo was married to
one of Wei's cousins. Cui was a Daoist—hence, the remark about Laozi's
teaching of *wu-wei,* "no effort."

74   In Reply to Gentleman-in-Attendance Chang Dang

I just happened to quit my post
and end up in the countryside
where the rising sun lights thatched huts
and gardens and groves support simple folk
though I'd agree I'm without means
my wine cup is rarely empty
I delight in ripening grain
and sigh at the work of creation
in step with villagers dawn to dusk
there's nothing they do I don't
I cut bamboo along the stream to the south
and return at night to the Feng's east shore
I retired because of incompetence
it wasn't to follow a higher path
I read your essay of jade and gold
its beautiful hues lit up my face
day after day I've wanted to reply
that was in spring and now it's winter

---

74 Written in the winter of 780 at Shanfu Hermitage on the Feng. The friend to whom Wei took so long to reply was working in the central government's Construction Commission at the time. He was also a well-known poet, and the men exchanged a number of poems.

76 Planting Melons

When I follow my nature I'm rash
too careless to earn a living
this year I tried planting melons
in a garden that was mostly weeds
the plants all shared the rain and dew
but mine ended up in the shade
and once spring work got busy
the time for hoeing was past
the farmers laughed at my useless efforts
from dawn to dusk with nothing to show
clearly this isn't my kind of work
I should stick with ancient texts instead

80 In Reply to My Nephew Zhao Kang

I recently left the woods and clouds
suddenly I'm in step with mandarins
I see the mountains but I can't leave
and I know you're there waiting for me

[76] Written in the spring of 781 at his hermitage on the Feng. Wei recalls the official who lost his position and became famous for his melons.

[80] Written in the summer of 781 after Wei accepted a post at court in Chang'an. High officials were likened to mandarin ducks, as they wore ornate robes and attended court in pairs. His nephew, however, is "there" at the family home near the foot of the Zhongnan Mountains.

91　Meeting Secretary Lu Geng of Luoyang in Yangzhou

In the land of Chu friends are rare
meeting you here was unexpected
I've kept your letters close to my heart
how strange to see white in your hair
our cups overflow with an innkeeper's wine
our luggage is full of river-travel poems
may we ride forth together again
as we once did on Luoyang Bridge

95　New Fall Night: To My Cousins

Our two worlds share this autumn night
we see the same river of stars
a leaf drops from a towering paulownia
thoughts of going home fill my rooms
I worry about the hardships of the people
then too I have my own minor ills
I won't be leaving anytime soon
but my hairline has already slipped away

[91] Written in the early fall of 782 while stopping in Yangzhou on the way to his new post in Chuzhou. Both towns were in the ancient state of Chu.

[95] Written in the fall of 782 in Chuzhou while watching the full moon and Milky Way. Once one paulownia leaf drops, the rest aren't far behind.

106   For Attendant Li Dan

There's not much excitement in a country town
I went to see spring in Guangling
the fading flowers still welcomed my visit
and no one asked who was in my heart

110   Chuzhou's West Stream

I love unnoticed plants that grow beside a stream
orioles singing overhead somewhere in the trees
at dusk the current quickens fed by springtime rains
I pull myself across on an unmanned country ferry

---

[106] Written in the late spring of 783. Bored in Chuzhou, Wei visited Yang-zhou (Guangling), which was the administrative headquarters for the district of which Chuzhou was a part. The "fading flowers" indicate late spring, but they also suggest a visit involving female entertainers.

[110] Written in the spring of 783 in Chuzhou. After spending the day wandering around the countryside, Wei returned so late he had to pull himself across the stream on the cable boat kept there for that purpose.

116 In Reply to Vice Director for Ceremonials Yang

With so many ills and a provincial assignment
I'm glad to receive honored guests
if no one visits for three or four days
it seems like months on end
wine loses its taste when I drink alone
I notice the dust on the facing seat
but once I'm in a boat singing
and a sprinkling of snow turns everything new
the mist and waves beg for an outing
the scenery is all on display
autumn ponds dotted with leaves
countryside temples no one else visits
filling out records is such a waste of effort
writing when I'm free is better
the sky is clear and the lake pavilion peaceful
chrysanthemums are blooming in the cold
it's time you got out that oar
and came back and showed me how you feel

[116] Written in the fall of 783 in Chuzhou. The vice director of ceremonials
was in charge of court rituals and also guided visitors in proper decorum.
Rather than rowing a boat with two oars, the Chinese have traditionally
used a single oar, or scull, at the stern.

118   Retired Living: To My Cousins

When plants in the courtyard bloom in the frost
I think about my cousins in our garden even more
all day in my fine quarters with nothing to do
I write poems on banana tree leaves

124   Climbing a Tower: To Councillor Wang

I hate climbing mountains and towers without you
the clouds the waters of Chu and memories never end
the sound of mallets at the foot of leafless hills
a prefecture of brambles in winter rain

[118] Written in the fall of 783 in Chuzhou. Although the title suggests otherwise, Wei is still serving as magistrate—just not a very busy one. Chrysanthemums are the plants most commonly associated with autumn and also with old age. The first frost usually occurs about the time they begin blooming. In the last line, Wei recalls the calligrapher-monk Huaisu, who used banana leaves when he didn't have paper handy.

[124] Written in the early winter of 783 in Chuzhou. Councillor Wang visited Wei but had since returned to Chang'an. Chuzhou was once in the eastern part of the ancient state of Chu, the name of which means "brambles." People beat clothes with mallets in fall to flatten the fabric in preparation for winter winds.

129   For Master Zong

Ever since the master's visit
paperwork has piled up on my desk
getting away takes a special occasion
but noise and quiet are both Zen
relaxing by the garden pond in late spring
sleeping on a clear night in my room upstairs
I can't catch a thing with this Dao
I'd be better off if I forgot the trap

130   To Li Dan and Yuan Xi

We met and parted last year among flowers
a year later they're blooming again
human affairs are too uncertain to predict
spring is so depressing I fall asleep alone
illness plagues my body and my thoughts are in the fields
I'm ashamed of my salary with refugees in town
I heard you were planning to come for a visit
how many moons have I watched from West Tower

[129] Written in the spring of 784 in Chuzhou. The last couplet refers to Zhuangzi's advice to forget the trap once the fish is caught. (*Zhuangzi* 26.11)

[130] Chuzhou's West Tower looked out on the road that led to the capital, which was occupied by rebels at this time. The refugees were from the towns in between.

131   To My Cousins

Late last year when the capital was being looted
I sent letters by back roads to see if you survived
your answer has suddenly fallen from the sky
all we know of one another are a thousand streams of tears

133   To Hengcan

My thoughts were free of past and future
I left worldly affairs behind
I followed a path through autumn grass
and spent a cold night at a mountain temple
today in my quarters with nothing to do
I'm thinking of asking about the *Lankavatara*

---

[131] Written in the summer of 784 in Chuzhou. In a note to this poem, Wei
says he sent a messenger to the Tang court at its temporary headquarters
in Fengtian in the tenth month of 783, along with letters to his family and
friends. The messenger returned in the fifth month of 784.

[133] Written in the fall of 784 in Chuzhou. Hengcan was a monk who
lived on nearby Langyashan and with whom Wei exchanged a number of
poems. The *Lankavatara* was the sutra most often used for instruction by
early Zen masters in China. Its primary teaching is that everything is noth-
ing but mind, and any division between thinker and thought is illusory.

136   Hearing Wild Geese

My old garden is somewhere in the distance
thoughts of going home never stop
on a rainy fall night in Huainan
from my room upstairs I hear geese

137   Eating Solomon's Seal

This magic herb comes from the hills to the west
for the edible part I use the root
steaming it nine times transforms it
that is what the old texts say
I tend the fire starting at midnight
its fragrance fills the south study
fasting brings out its powers
herbal arts unlock its mysteries
the thoughts I cherish of transcendence
aren't something I discuss with worldly people
someday I plan to give up this career
and live forever with Heaven and Earth

---

[136] Written in the fall of 784 in Chuzhou. Thoughts are going north, geese are heading south.

[137] Written in the fall of 784 in Chuzhou. Solomon's seal is collected in the fall and used to lighten the body and extend one's years. Wei took his own advice and resigned a few months later—if only for a while.

138 New Year's Day: To My Cousins, Including Duan and Wu, in the Capital

With deep disappointment I face the year
an émigré wondering how to get home
troubled to be apart from those I love
feeling the drag of a worldly career
I served in Heyang when I was young
in old age I've been guarding the shores of Huainan
how many times have we parted this life
and now we've reached our useless years
yesterday I turned in my seal of office
but poverty has forced me to stay on
most of the battalions have left
and transport is in poor supply
drink is my companion now that I'm retired
I cultivate the Dao in silence
I listen to the pines at South Cliff Temple
and watch the moon in West Creek
there's no secret to government work
just do your job and don't expect a transfer
I'm finally packing the clothes I brought
I'm going home to work those Duling fields

---

[138] Written on the first day of 785 in Chuzhou. Wei lived at South Cliff Temple after resigning. West Creek was next to it. The Duling Plateau was the location of the Wei family home and where his cousins lived.

143 On First Reaching This Prefecture

Pencheng is an ancient and strategic town
straddling a river that races a thousand miles
tall trees tower overhead
steep parapets wind around
neighborhoods fill with kitchen smoke at dusk
every plant and tree in the countryside is green
an ocean of water surges past the north wall
a lofty ridge rises beyond the south rampart
people here once loved life
so why have they run away
after years of drought and poor harvests
their unpaid taxes form hills
I've been in this prefecture more than a month
today I finally cleared up the mess
but acquaintances haven't come by for dinner
and I'm already bored with reports
worthies of the past rode a higher wind
I'm embarrassed to serve in such a meaningless post
do I have to wait for warfare to end
before comforting widows and orphans

[143] Written in the late summer of 785 upon reaching his new post as magistrate of Jiangzhou, or modern Jiujiang, which was also called Pencheng. During Wei's tenure, warfare caused by the revolt of the separatist governor Li Xilie, who controlled the Huai River watershed to the north, forced many people to become refugees.

144 Climbing the City Tower: To My Cousins in the Capital and My Nephews in Huainan

I recently quit my post in Yongyang
already I'm lounging in Xunyang Tower
a cold rain spatters the balcony railing
the steep parapet juts into the Yangzi
I've heard wild geese at night since arriving
I keep recalling our autumn goodbyes
the wine in this cup doesn't work
diluted by so many cares

149 While Observing Local Customs, I Visited My Daoist Nephew without Success and Wrote This on His Wall

Last year's mountain stream is still flowing today
last year's apricot blossoms I picked again today
a hermit on the trail asked me who I am
I'm the same spring visitor as last year

---

[144] Written in the fall of 785 in Jiangzhou. Yongyang was another name for Chuzhou and Xunyang an old name for Jiangzhou. The city wall was built along the south shore of the Yangzi, and the tower on which Wei stood was built out into the river. After leaving Chuzhou, Wei visited his nephews in Yangzhou before sailing up the Yangzi to Jiangzhou.

[149] Written at the beginning of 787 in Jiangzhou. Officials were required to tour their administrative regions at the new year. Here, Wei visited nearby Lushan and, failing to find his nephew, left this poem behind.

150 Spring Thoughts

Snow white wildflowers surround this river town
seeing their annual blooms I recall the royal city
the palace gates at dawn opening on trees of jade
standing beside the mandarins listening to orioles

162 Thinking of the Past at Changmen Gate

A lone bird lands on a towering tree
having heard from afar of the gardens of Wu
and lamenting the history of a thousand years
I lean at sunset against Changmen Gate

[150] Written in the early spring of 787 in Jiangzhou. Wei recalls his days at court when he served in the palace guard. Mandarin ducks refer to officials, who entered the palace in pairs wearing ornate robes. Orioles are associated with early spring and also with those who give honest advice that goes unheeded.

[162] Written in the spring of 789 shortly after Wei arrived in Suzhou to serve as its new magistrate. Changmen Gate was an old name for the city's West Gate. This was the gate from which the armies of the ancient state of Wu marched forth during the first millennium BCE. Suzhou is still China's most famous garden city. Wei combines the history of the state of Wu here with that of the Tang dynasty and his own life.

165 Autumn Night: To Supernumerary Qiu Twenty-Two

Out walking and singing of cooler days
I think of you this autumn night
pinecones falling on deserted slopes
the recluse I suspect not yet asleep

166 The Ninth

Suddenly I'm administering Wu Prefecture
and suddenly chrysanthemums are blooming
as I start to think of my garden back home
happily a group of guests arrives

[165] Written in the fall of 789 in Suzhou. Qiu Dan served briefly as Wei's secretary but decided he would rather cultivate the Dao. Hence, he retired to a hermitage on Pingshan, outside Yangzhou. Since this was the eighth full moon, when relatives and friends normally spend the night together, Wei tries to imagine how lonely his friend must feel.

[166] Written on the ninth day of the ninth month of 789 in Suzhou. Wu Prefecture was another name for Suzhou, as it was once the capital of the ancient state of Wu.

167 Hearing a Flute on the River
While Seeing Off Censor Lu

Seeing you off over cups of wine
in the distance I heard a flute on the water
spending the night alone is sad enough
without hearing it again in my quarters

169 Visiting Kaiyuan Hermitage

Wearing summer clothes makes me feel lighter
I love following trails to monastic retreats
to an orchard of fruit trees after a rain
or a terrace of incense lit by the dawn
where green shade nurtures quiet days
or a solitary blossom is the last sign of spring
my official duties have kept me so busy
my footsteps have come here too seldom

[167] Written in the early winter of 789 in Suzhou. Censor Lu, or Lu Can, was a native of Suzhou but was stationed in Shaoxing, to which he was returning via the Grand Canal.

[169] Written in the early summer of 790 after resigning his post as magistrate of Suzhou. Kaiyuan Temple was just outside Suzhou.

175 At Yongding Temple Biqiang Happily Arrives at Night

You came with New Year greetings
walking here alone in the bitter cold
knocking on a bamboo temple gate at night
covered with snow from your hike through the hills
I started a fire from the embers in the stove
and closed the door to my empty room
we shared a gourd full of wine
and didn't speak of all the things that went wrong

[175] Written at the beginning of 791 at the temple, beyond Suzhou's West Gate, to which he had retired. Zhao Biqiang was one of Wei's nephews. Wei stopped writing poems after this one; he died a short while later.

FINDING THEM GONE

Finding Them Gone

I'm a pilgrim at heart, happiest when I'm on a trail, following signs left by someone I'd like to meet. I never realized this until I wondered whether there really were recluses like Cold Mountain and Stonehouse. I thought maybe it was simply a Chinese literary conceit. And when I found dozens of men and women in the mountains of China following the Dao and the Dharma, I felt someone might like to know. So I wrote a book titled *Road to Heaven: Encounters with Chinese Hermits*. I never planned to write another one. I thought of myself as a translator. And being a translator, I naturally needed a day job.

I worked at ICRT, an English-language radio station in Taiwan, from 1981 until 1989. It was formerly operated by the Armed Forces Network, but the US abandoned it when Washington recognized Beijing as the rightful seat of the government of China. The station had a huge following in Taiwan, not just among foreigners but also locals, who found listening a great way to improve their English. So a nonprofit was created with a board made up of prominent Western and Taiwanese business leaders, and I was hired to translate stories from the local press and to do interviews. That was the job I quit in order to look for hermits.

Just as I was finishing the manuscript, my old boss was hired to set up Hong Kong's first private, English-language station in 1991, and he asked me to join him. My job, he said, would be to produce a daily two-minute feature. I had never done anything like that, but I had an idea. I had planned to return to America when I finished the hermit manuscript and had always wanted to explore the origins of Chinese culture, so I called up Winston Wong, the head of Formosa Plastics. I had interviewed him before, and he had supported my trip to find Chinese hermits. I asked him if he would support another trip, this time along the Yellow River. All he wanted to know was whether I wanted cash or traveler's checks. And so I had a mission and funding, and my boss thought it was worth trying. When I returned to Hong Kong two months later, I produced 240 two-minute pieces about my journey from the mouth of the Yellow River to its source. It was a huge success among Hong Kong listeners, and I followed that with journeys on the Silk Road—from Xi'an to Islamabad, among the hill tribes of Southwest China, and through the cultural region known as South of the Yangzi.

Two years later, the job ended, and I returned to America and went back to translating Buddhist texts and poetry. But the pilgrimage karma wouldn't go away. One day I got this harebrained idea to pour whiskey on the graves of the poets whose poems I had been translating. Who would have guessed that the Guggenheim Foundation would give me the money to do exactly that? What follows are three short excerpts from what came to be *Finding Them Gone,* whose title I borrowed from Chinese poetry—failing to find someone home but writing about the experience anyway.

WANG WEI 王維

I was out on the street before eight, which I thought would be early enough. But I was already late. I hadn't reckoned with the morning traffic. I was half a dozen blocks away from the chaos surrounding Xi'an's Bell Tower, but I still couldn't find a taxi. I kept walking from one street corner to the next. Finally, I saw one stop on the other side of the street to deliver its passengers. I dodged cars and buses and managed to jump inside before anyone else.

I told the driver we were going to the countryside. I figured that would cheer him up. Who wants to be stuck in traffic? But we were stuck—and heading the wrong direction. At least it was a beginning. It took forty-five minutes to reach the expressway that ringed the city and another thirty to reach the G70 Expressway that led southeast toward the Zhongnan Mountains. It was one of three such roads from Xi'an that had been built in recent years not only to the mountains but through them, thus joining the central part of Shaanxi Province with its heretofore remote southern part.

The G70 soon merged with the G40, and we found ourselves nearly alone. After the congestion of the city, it was like flying above the clouds. Xi'an was behind us. A few minutes later, the town of Lantian was behind us too. A few minutes after that, we were in the mountains, literally, as we began passing through one tunnel after another. It was as if the road said, "Out of my way, mountains." After ten kilometers, we exited at the village of Wangchuan and switched to the old road that had carried more than a few poets into exile. I had been on it once before, in 1989. There were only a few scattered farms then and nothing worth calling a village. Despite the beauty of the valley the Wang River had carved out of the mountains, it was simply too remote, even for farmers. But things had changed. The old road that followed the river upstream was now lined with weekend getaways for the government bureaucrats and office workers who served the new rulers of Xi'an.

After several kilometers, we began stopping to ask directions for Baijiaping 白家坪. The place I was looking for wasn't far, and the third person we asked said it was just around the next bend, which it was. From the main road, we turned left onto a narrower road and a minute later drove through a gate that should have been closed. Two hundred meters later, we pulled up just short of the huge ginkgo tree that led me here. It was planted by the poet Wang Wei (d. 761). This was the site of his Wang River Retreat, a tract of land previously owned by the poet Song Zhiwen (d. 710).

Among the attractions Wang maintained on the property was a large fenced-in area where he kept deer. He called it Deer Park, in honor of the place in India where the Buddha gave his first sermon. The poem he wrote with that as its title was one of his most famous:

> Deserted mountain no sign of people
> except for the sound of their voices

> as sunlight shone through the trees again
> it illuminated the green moss once more

That third line puzzled people, even Chinese readers. It turns out the place it describes is a very narrow east–west valley, where the sunlight slips under the trees early and also late in the day, but not in between.

The first time I visited Wang River, I was also looking for Wang Wei's valley. But I went looking in the valley just north of it. After several hours in the mountains, I was hiking back down with my photographer friend Steve Johnson, when we were arrested by military police and taken back to Xi'an for interrogation. Fortunately, we saw them before they saw us, and Steve was able to hide his film in his socks and put new film in his camera for them to expose later. We were saved on that occasion by our obvious stupidity. Later, a friend whose job it was to analyze satellite photos for the CIA pointed out that the peculiar apparatus along a stream in one of Steve's photos was a high-capacity heat-sink used to reduce temperatures involved in the manufacture of such things as warheads. This confirmed what I had overheard from the military police about why we shouldn't have been there. They didn't know I spoke Chinese, and I did nothing to disabuse them of that impression. But that was twenty-three years ago. The thought never occurred to me that nothing had changed.

Workers in blue uniforms were standing around the tree on a smoke break. When I got out of the taxi, one of them told me I shouldn't be there. But no one did anything. Their break was over, and they walked back into a huge metal building next to the mountainside. I took a few photos of the tree with my two cameras, a digital one and one with black-and-white slide film. I thought about continuing on into the valley, which appeared to end about two or three hundred meters farther on. That was where Wang Wei's home and Deer Park Temple, which later replaced it, were once located. I decided I'd better not press my luck and returned to my taxi. We headed back toward the gate, but we didn't make it through. Three men ran out of the building next to the gate and motioned for us to stop. They were military officers of some kind, but they were all wearing civilian clothes. One of them ordered a uniformed guard standing just inside the gate to close and padlock it. Then they began questioning my driver.

I got out and asked what was wrong, as if I didn't know. When the man who seemed to be in charge asked me what I was doing there, I told him I was there to pay my respects to Wang Wei. Not only was the ginkgo he planted still there, so was his grave, in a manner of speaking, underneath the abandoned brick building that was formerly the Xiangyang Munitions Factory, now dwarfed by two new metal buildings.

The officer asked me if I had taken any photographs. I told him I had but only of the ginkgo and the sign next to it that said this tree was planted by Wang Wei. I told him I was writing a book about visiting the graves and homes of

China's most famous poets of the past and was hoping to include a photo of Wang Wei's tree. He and the other officers conferred for a few minutes. Then the officer in charge took out his cellphone and made a call. After he had spoken with someone, he told me to give him my camera. I reached into my arm bag and took out the digital one. I had bought it only the year before and wasn't that familiar with the buttons. I knew how to take pictures and how to download them onto a computer. That was about it.

After I handed him the camera, he turned it on and reviewed my photos. One by one, he deleted all those I had just taken. Then he handed it back to me. That surprised me. I thought he was going to delete everything. As I put the camera back into my arm bag, he said the area was off-limits to everyone, to Chinese as well as foreigners. I apologized for my ignorance. But before getting back into the taxi, I asked him if he could take a picture of the tree for me, one that would not include the buildings. He conferred with his fellow officers again then said, "No." The area was off-limits. No photos. I told him I had seen a photo of the tree on the Internet. But that didn't sway him. It was clearly time to leave. I thanked him, and he told the guard to unlock the gate.

Once we returned to the main road, we retraced our way back to where we exited the expressway earlier. This time I told the driver to stay on the old road, the one that followed the river downstream. After a kilometer or two, just before the river entered a gorge, I asked him to pull over. I wanted to share some bourbon with Wang Wei. The driver was only too happy to stop. The incident had left him visibly shaken. I walked down to the shore where the river made a wide bend before it narrowed. At a suitable spot, I set out a cup for Wang Wei and another for his friend Bei Di. I sat down on a boulder and watched the water ripple over the rocks. It was along this shore that Wang Wei painted his famous Wang River Scroll, to which he and Bei Di added a series of poems. Wang Wei's "Deer Park" was on the scroll. Another one was "Bamboo Retreat":

> Sitting alone amid dense bamboo
> strumming my zither and droning
> deep in the forest no one else knows
> until the bright moon looks down

Wang Wei wasn't only a poet, he was also a musician, and he could drone, much like the Tuvan throat singers still do. He was a talented man. He even rose to the post of deputy prime minister. But his heart was in the mountains. He called himself Layman Vimalakirti, after the interlocutor of the Buddhist sutra of the same name. Whenever he wasn't needed in the capital, this was where he came to meditate, to drone, to play music, to paint, to hike, and to do nothing at all. It must have been hard for him to go back to town. After sipping some of the whiskey I had set out for him and his friend, I recited the poem he titled "On Leaving My Wang River Retreat":

With reluctance I readied my horse and carriage
sadly the tree moss is now behind me
I can bear leaving the blue mountains
but what about the green water

What I didn't finish, I poured into the green water and left Wang Wei to his river. By the time I got back to the taxi, the driver was his old self. The trauma of the warhead factory was probably going to be just another story he would tell his wife that night over dinner.

DU MU 杜牧

On our way back to Xi'an, as we approached the city, I asked the driver to turn right onto Changan East Road. The road ran along the northern edge of a plateau, and we followed it, as well as its narrower successor. When it ended at Highway 113, we turned southeast, back toward the mountains. Five kilometers later, we came to the village of Tongxiang and started stopping to ask farmers the way to Sima Village. The third farmer knew where it was and pointed us south. Two kilometers later, we were there.

It wasn't much of a village, maybe two hundred meters on a side. Halfway through, I asked the driver to stop. I got out and approached an old man. He was sitting on a stool repairing his mattock and smoking what looked like a hand-rolled cigar. I asked him if he knew where Du Mu (d. 852) was buried. I always liked to ask questions like that—about someone who lived a thousand or more years ago. And I always enjoyed the response. In this case, the old man simply nodded and got up and led me behind the cluster of mud-brick houses that made up the village. As we walked along, I looked at his cigar. It consisted of a single tobacco leaf, which was, I guess, what a cigar was. As he led me out into a field, several other villagers joined us. They were all smoking the same kind of cigar. Apparently, tobacco was one of the local crops. After walking a hundred meters or so through fields of beans then eggplant then corn and finally onions, the old man stopped and pointed to a pit at the edge of an unplanted field. He said that was where the grave used to be. He said some officials came there in the 1970s and took away whatever it was they dug up. He said they hadn't been back. The pit was all that remained, and it was full of trash. Apparently, the villagers whose houses were nearby found it a convenient place to throw stuff they didn't want before they burned it.

Du Mu was one of the few major poets of the Tang born and raised in Chang'an. But once he passed the civil service exam, he spent most of his career far from the capital. As he was getting ready to leave to take up his final post, he wrote "Climbing Leyou Plateau Before Leaving for Wuxing":

The times might be peaceful but not for me
I envy the freedom of clouds and the stillness of monks
about to take my banner to the shores of the Yangzi
from Leyou Plateau I look toward Zhaoling

Zhaoling was the name of the tomb of Emperor Taizong (d. 649), the founder of the Tang dynasty. From the plateau just north of his village, it would have been visible as a bump on the north horizon. When Du Mu wrote this poem, it was not a peaceful time—his first line is facetious. But his admiration of Taizong was genuine. Taizong was an astute judge of men, and as Du Mu sees his career winding down, he regrets not having served such a ruler. He was always writing to his friends at court to suggest policies they should be following, or at least promoting. He died shortly after returning from this last assignment and was buried at the edge of the village in what had since become the village trash pit.

I filled a cup with bourbon, took a sip, and poured the rest into the pit. Then I took out a copy of his most famous poem and read it aloud. It was about graves and spirits and was titled "Purification Day." In Confucius's day, this day in early April was celebrated by bathing in a river. By Du Mu's time, it had become a day for visiting the graves of one's ancestors. But the day he wrote this poem, Du Mu was nowhere near the family cemetery. He was traveling along a road near the Yangzi town of Guichi:

> Purification Day and the rain pours down
> a traveler on the road feels his heart sink
> where can he buy some wine he asks
> a herd boy points to Apricot Blossom Village

The farmers standing beside me all knew the poem by heart. By the time I made it to the second line, they all had joined me. They had probably memorized it in elementary school. I poured another cup and offered it to the farmer who led me there. He took a sip, and his eyes widened. He handed it back and took another drag on his cigar. He said something to his fellow farmers, and they all laughed. It was dialect. Although I didn't understand, I didn't doubt it concerned the bourbon. It was 142 proof. I poured the rest into what was once Du Mu's grave and smiled at the thought. Apricot Flower Village was, and still is, famous for its white lightning. It resuscitated Du Mu that day nearly 1,200 years ago. I don't know if the George T. Stagg reached him that day or not, but his poem reached us in the village where he was buried. I thanked the old man for showing me where his grave used to be and walked back to the taxi.

Su Dongpo 蘇東坡

Another day, another poet. Today it was Su Dongpo (d. 1101). Su was not only one of China's greatest poets, he was also one of its greatest essayists and calligraphers as well as one of the most prominent political figures of his time, leading the opposition at court to the economic reforms introduced by prime minister and fellow poet Wang Anshi. It was his opposition that resulted in a series of exiles, the first of which was to the Yangzi river town of Huanggang (ancient Huangzhou). That was my destination for the day, and an early morning train from Wuhan carried me downriver to Ezhou, just across the river from Su's place of exile.

Su was forty-three when he and his wife arrived. It was shortly afterward that he started using the name Dongpo, meaning "East Slope," as it was the name of the piece of land he and his wife began farming to make ends meet. Up until then, he was simply Su Shi 蘇軾. Ezhou was not a major stop, and I was lucky to find a taxi waiting outside the station. I asked the driver to take me to the Su Dongpo Memorial Hall. His exile was the most famous thing that ever happened in Huanggang. Fifteen minutes later, I arrived at the city's effort to honor him. It was a new building and had that Song-dynasty look, everything either white or black. It was an elegant look. The exhibits inside were new, too, and a welcome change from the standard glass cases. It looked like someone had taken a course in museum management. The emphasis was on dioramas and audiovisual displays.

As I walked into the main hall, over the loudspeaker Deng Lijun was singing "I Can Only Hope as Long as We Live." It was her rendition of Su's famous "Water Tune Song," a poem he wrote to his brother:

> How many moons do we have
> lifting my cup I asked the sky
> in the palaces above I wonder
> what year it is tonight
> I wish I could ride there on the wind
> but I fear those towers of jade

may be too high and cold for me
and dancing in those icy shadows
no match for here on earth

As it rolls past painted gates
and silken windows below
it lights those not asleep
I shouldn't bear it ill will
but why is it always full when we part
we have our goodbyes and reunions
the moon too waxes and wanes
being together has always been rare
I can only hope as long as we live
Chang'e bridges the miles between us

Chang'e is the name of the goddess who lives in a palace on the moon, where she dispenses pills that make mortals immortal. In Huanggang, Deng Lijun had taken her place. Even though Deng was from Taiwan, she was just as popular on the Mainland, despite the government's refusal to allow her music to be sold openly—it was considered too bourgeois. Still, there was a saying in China in those days (the '80s and '90s): "Deng Xiaoping rules the day, but Deng Lijun rules the night." A lot had changed in thirty years— and a lot hadn't.

As I entered a series of galleries, Deng's voice faded in the distance. The first gallery consisted of photos of places around China where Su had lived—and he lived in a lot of places. There were also photos of his and his brother's graves, where I had shared some bourbon earlier on my pilgrimage; but a photo of another grave surprised me. I had visited it before and even conducted a ceremony there on a friend's behalf. It was the grave of his wife, Wang Zhaoyun. Su bought her out of indentured servitude when she was twelve, and she soon became his constant companion. She died in Huizhou, not far from Hong Kong, during Su's final exile. Su said she died chanting the poem that ends the *Diamond Sutra:*

> As a lamp a cataract a star in space
> an illusion a dewdrop a bubble
> a dream a cloud a flash of lightning
> view all created things like this

Her devotion to the Dharma had a great effect on Su. She was only eighteen when they arrived in Huanggang, but it was during his stay here that he took up meditation and the study of such Buddhist sutras as the *Diamond,* the *Vimalakirti,* even the *Lankavatara.*

Past the gallery of photos was another consisting of dioramas depicting scenes from Su's life in the city. My favorite was of him and his wife going over their budget to figure how to get by on his meager salary. There were also plasticized examples of the culinary skills he developed in Huanggang and the dishes named for him: Dongpo Fish, Dongpo Pork, Dongpo Doufu, Dongpo Chowder, even Dongpo Cookies.

On one of the walls was a scroll by the thirteenth-century calligrapher Xian Yushu. It was Su's poem "Crabapple," about a tree near his house in Huanggang and the arrival of spring:

> The wafting east wind the rays of sublime light
> as the moon crossed the porch perfume filled the air
> worried the night was late and its flowers about to sleep
> I held up a candle to see its red attire

Other than me, only a woman caretaker was at the memorial hall; she knitted the whole time I was there. That was what caretakers did in the old days. Now they send text messages. Suddenly a group of VIPs arrived, and just as suddenly an official appeared out of nowhere and gave them a guided tour. It was a whirlwind tour and over in less than ten minutes. Lunch was clearly on their agenda, and, no doubt, on someone else's tab. I continued to linger over the dioramas. They were done so well. There was also one of Su playing his zither, and a calligraphic rendering of his "Zither Poem":

> You say the zither's sound comes from its strings
> then why doesn't it play in its case
> you say the sound comes from the fingers
> then why are yours silent

But best of all was a model of the Song-dynasty city with all the places inside and outside the walls marked where Su lived and wrote. Huanggang, of course, had changed, but the old walls were, for the most part, intact. There was an interactive display, and I reached out and pulled on a pair of oars. Suddenly I was on the Yangzi rowing past Red Cliff. There was even a recording of oars dipping into the river. How could I resist? I had to go to the cliff.

I exited the hall and walked to where the taxi driver had dropped me off. Just before I got there, I stopped. Carved on a huge stone edifice were inscriptions of Su's "Red Cliff Odes" with reliefs of him out on the river. I couldn't wait to join him. But when I turned my attention to finding a taxi, I discovered Huanggang was not a taxi town. All I saw were buses and private cars. I could have taken a bus. But place names were always a mystery in a town I had never been in before. I stuck with the taxi option. It took twenty minutes, but one finally pulled up to deliver three more memorial hall visitors. I asked the driver to take me to Red Cliff, and we were there in ten minutes. It was so close, I could have walked. But I'm glad I didn't. This was supposed to be an easy day.

When I got out, I was surprised. I was expecting a cliff next to the river. The cliff was still there, just outside the city's old west wall, as it had always been, but it no longer overlooked the Yangzi. It was now behind a dike. There was also a large pond between the cliff and the dike. Apparently, the pond was designed to make the cliff feel better about being landlocked and twenty meters shorter—which was what I estimated the difference between the water levels of the pond and the Yangzi to be. Although Red Cliff had lost some of its height, it was still a cliff, and I walked over for a closer look.

This was where Su rowed out into the Yangzi one night in 1082, with several friends and a jug of wine, and wrote his two "Red Cliff Odes." In the first, he lamented the impermanence of the ever-flowing river and the ever-changing moon, then laughed in praise of their inexhaustible presence. In the second, he fell asleep drunk only to wake and look in vain for the crane that flew above him in his dream before transforming itself into a Daoist immortal.

When I reached a place opposite the cliff, I set three cups on a rock near the shore for Su and his boatmates and filled them with rye. I decided on rye instead of bourbon for this part of my pilgrimage. It was another grain that never made it to China until modern times. Representing this noble grain was Thomas H. Handy. Nothing but the best for my poet friends. At 128 proof, I felt confident it would have produced similar results a thousand years earlier.

While I was taking in the view and waiting for the spirits to commune, it started to rain—at first I thought it was just minnows rising to the surface. As I sipped my share of the rainwater and rye, I changed my mind about the place. At first I didn't like the cliff being separated from the river. But after a while, the place grew on me. At the far end of the pond was a stand of last year's lotuses, desiccated and bent, waiting to collapse into the mud and make way for new ones. Along the bank, willow catkins were just beginning to turn green. In the distance, I heard firecrackers announcing another transition in life. I could imagine more odes being written about impermanence and its inexhaustible presence. After emptying what I didn't finish into the pond, I read Su the poem he titled "Fish":

> I released some minnows into the lake
> newly hatched and unafraid
> once they learn about hooks
> I'll never see them again

Would that it were true, I thought. As I walked back to the park entrance, a large fish did a belly flop. Apparently, the rain was bringing insects down to the surface. I was glad I remembered my umbrella.

ZHU SHUZHEN 朱淑貞

None of us—not our driver, or Mr. Lin, or my tea brother Dacha—had been to where I hoped to go, so it took a while. But we persevered. There were so many new roads being built in China. Finally, we arrived at our destination: Luchong, the hometown of Zhu Shuzhen (d. 1180).

Of China's women poets, she was my favorite. The town where she was born was a canal town. Most of the canal towns had been leveled for factories or turned into tourist attractions, but Luchong was an exception, if only because it was so small. Since its stone-lined streets weren't wide enough for cars, we parked just inside the southwest corner, then walked along the ancient cobblestone road that ran parallel to the town's main canal. The two-story houses on both sides of the narrow street were made of wood; the upper stories on the canal side extended over the waterway, and red lanterns hung from the eaves. On the street side, it was simple but picturesque.

After walking a hundred meters, we crossed a stone bridge. After another fifty, we came to Zhenxi Road No. 38, the Zhu Shuzhen Exhibition Hall. It was easily the nicest building in the village. Someone in Luchong clearly loved her. Not only was the building in good condition, the design of the exhibits inside was also well done. Her poems lined the walls, as did photographs of scenes around the village. I had read about the hall online, and I expected to find books of her poetry for sale, but there weren't any. Nor was there anyone to guide us or regale us with stories only a person from Luchong would know.

After reading the poems and explanations, I walked back outside. There was a small dry-goods store across the street run by an old couple, and I thought maybe they had books for sale. They didn't, but the man surprised me. He suggested I have a look at Zhu Shuzhen's old house. I didn't know it had survived. The man said to go back the way we had come, turn right, then left, then right. Sounded simple. Her house, he said, was next to a pavilion that overlooked another canal. Five minutes later, I returned and asked him whether he could guide me. I must have taken a left when I should have taken a right. He hadn't been there in a while himself, but he agreed. He was ninety-one and had to retrace his steps several times, but he found it. After telling the people who lived in the building what I was doing, he went back to his store.

It was a fairly large and very old structure, and it was occupied by several families. The residents were quite friendly and invited me in, but I didn't feel like intruding. A few minutes later, Dacha and Mr. Lin also found their way there. While they talked to the residents, I walked around back to the pavilion that overlooked a much smaller canal. I could imagine Zhu sitting there in spring writing "Events on a Spring Day":

It's teeth-clenching cold and the flowers are late
green ripple upon ripple joins the distant waves
fish rise from river grass showing off their jade flanks
orioles weave through trees like shuttles made of gold
I look through drafts of my poems by the sill
and listen to fishermen singing across the shore
all day by the window my heart beats in silence
with nothing here to do how will I survive spring

In ancient China, women were called *nei-ren,* "interior persons." They lived inside, behind the walls, where their lives were likewise "interior."

After my companions joined me at the pavilion, we walked over to the bridge that spanned the canal behind her house. It was the perfect place for our respective ceremonies. Dacha got out his tea, and I did the same with my whiskey. After thanking Zhu for her poems, we poured what we didn't drink into the water. I would have liked to have lingered but, as usual, I wasn't done for the day. Dacha and Mr. Lin dropped me off at the Dongxiang train station, which we'd passed on the way. Fifteen minutes later, I was on a bullet train. Thirty minutes after that, I got off in Hangzhou, the town where Zhu Shuzhen spent the second half of her life, the married half.

Before I knew it, it was my turn in the taxi queue. I told the driver the name of my hotel but added that I wanted to stop first in the old part of town. I wanted to walk down Zhongshan Middle Road. The street dated back to the Song dynasty, and its southern section had been fixed up to look as it might have nine hundred years ago, when Zhu was alive. According to an account I read online, her house was just off the pedestrian-only part of the street in Baokang Lane. While the taxi driver waited, I walked up and down Zhongshan Middle Road, but none of the shopkeepers had heard of Baokang Lane or Zhu Shuzhen's home. I gave up. But I wasn't done with Baokang Lane.

I happened to pass through Hangzhou a week later, the day before I flew back to Seattle. I had some time on my hands and wanted to walk down Zhongshan Middle Road once more. This time I got lucky. It turned out the account on the Internet had the first character of Baokang Lane wrong. It wasn't Precious Health Lane 寶康巷. It was Protecting Health Lane 保康巷. I could see how I had passed it by. It was barely wide enough to enter and less than fifty meters long. Just before the end of the lane, at No. 14, was

Zhu Shuzhen's old house. All the residents were distinctly proud of living in or next to or across from it. Apparently, the knowledge of its existence never made it to the street. Given the isolation that a failed marriage bestowed upon her, I imagine she was grateful for such a place and for the friendships that a city like Hangzhou made possible. I could see her writing "Around the Stove":

> Sitting around a glowing stove singing silly songs
> straining more new wine reciting more new poems
> none of us regretting getting drunk tonight
> this time won't come again once we say goodbye

But Protecting Health Lane was a week away, and I hadn't found it yet. The day was getting on, and I still had one more stop. I asked the driver to take me to my hotel and to wait while I divested myself of my bag. My Chinese friend Simeng was waiting in the lobby. She had offered to guide me to my final destination of the day: the Hangzhou Botanical Gardens.

It was only ten minutes from the hotel, but it was already after four when we walked through the main gate. The place closed at five thirty, so I walked faster than usual. I was trying to squeeze this last destination into the day because this was where Zhu Shuzhen was buried. People had written about visiting her grave. But the grave seems to have disappeared during the last century—at least until recently. Before beginning my trip, I read an online account by someone who claimed to have found her grave in the Lingfeng Tanmei section of the park. That part of the park was also one of Simeng's favorite places, which is why I asked her to be my guide. When I made up my itinerary, I knew I would be looking for Zhu's grave at the end of the day, in fading light, and couldn't afford a wrong turn.

In English, *ling-feng* means "spirit peak." The ridge that formed the western border of the park was known for its graves. And *tan-mei* means "looking for plum flowers." During the Song dynasty, when North China was lost to the nomadic Jurchens, the plum blossom came to represent the Chinese spirit of resilience. It bloomed when the weather was coldest. One of the many poems Zhu wrote on the subject was "I Send This Quatrain to the Poorly Located Plum Tree at the Foot of the Mountain Facing Away from the Sun and Finally Budding in Late Winter":

Plum buds are bursting near the store by the bridge
it's late winter in Hangzhou but still not cold enough
I'm sending this to the plum tree asking it to wait
without snow on your branches who is going to look

For Zhu Shuzhen, the plum flower represented not only the dynasty's resilience but also *her* resilience. She was a plum flower. That was why she asked to be buried here, where the people of Hangzhou came every year, especially after a snowfall, in search of plum blossoms.

After passing under a stone archway, we entered Looking

for Plum Blossoms Garden, then continued across a huge grassy bowl to the foot of Spirit Peak. It was November. The Lunar New Year was two months away, and the mountain's plum blossoms were still dreaming. As we walked along the foot of the mountain, we paused to read any and all inscriptions. But we saw nothing with Zhu's name on it. We kept walking and eventually followed a trail that led past dozens of thousand-year-old camphor trees. The trees were as old as Zhu's grave, if not older. Suddenly, I noticed that some of the paving stones we had been walking on were tombstones. I slowed down and looked more carefully.

I also kept looking at my watch. The park was about to close, and the light was fading from the sky. Finally, I called it quits. If I had stepped on her tombstone, I wouldn't have known. There wasn't enough light. As we headed back down the slope, I noticed several hundred narrow stone steps leading to the north side of the ridge. We were out of time, but I thought *what the hell* and started up. But halfway to the top, I stopped. I was out of breath and exhausted. I told Simeng I was turning back. But she urged me on, so I kept going, embarrassed that she was more determined than me. As we finally reached the top steps, *there* was the tombstone whose photo I had seen online. Whatever had been carved on its surface had been worn away by centuries of rain. Someone had scrawled some words on it with red paint. But they too had been mostly worn away. That someone had dared to write on a tombstone—there wasn't graffiti on any of the others—I took as confirmation that there was something special about this one. No doubt, the person who posted the photo felt the same. Whether it really was Zhu Shuzhen's grave didn't matter. This was her favorite place, and that was good enough for me.

Once I caught my breath, I took out the whiskey and thanked Zhu for her poems. They were hard-won, and we were fortunate to have them. Her parents were so embarrassed by her talent, they burned all the poems they could find after she died. Lucky for us, someone gathered copies she shared with friends, over three hundred of them, and titled the resulting collection *Poems of a Broken Heart*. It was an apt title. The only good thing about her marriage was that her husband left her alone. And the only good thing about her relationships with other men was that she survived them, except the last one. The most repeated story about her death was that she drowned herself in Hangzhou's West Lake after one heartbreak too many. But the truth is, all we really know is what we can find in her poems. And different people find different things.

By the time I was done thanking her with my little offering, the park gates had closed. Simeng said not to bother going back down and trying to climb the fence. She led me to a weather station above Zhu's grave, then along a dirt trail that wound past hundreds of Muslim graves, most of them dating back to the early twentieth century, when Hangzhou was called the "Stronghold of Islam" in China. It was nearly dark when we finally came off the hill and out to a street lined with fancy restaurants and brightly lit nightspots. It was a startling, unwelcome, change of scenery.

Fortunately, we were still on Simeng's turf, and she led me on a series of paths through hillsides of bamboo which circumvented the neon and the traffic and brought me back to my hotel. It was such an exhausting yet at the same time exhilarating day, I shared two bottles of wine with Simeng over dinner. Later that night, just before letting the day go, I read one more poem of Zhu's, "Looking for Plum Blossoms":

> The weather was so warm it could have been spring
> looking for plum blossoms I found a whole slope
> breaking off a twig and sticking it in my hair
> I laughed and asked *is anyone more shameless*

Certainly no one I knew.

Liu Zongyuan

LIU ZONGYUAN 柳宗元

When I applied to the Guggenheim Foundation to share some whiskey with China's greatest poets, Liu Zongyuan was not on my list. It wasn't because he didn't drink; it was because he was one of China's greatest essayists, not poets. But when the Guggenheim surprised me by approving my request, and I started planning my trip in earnest, I discovered that several of the poets on the list ranked Liu as one of the four greatest poets of the Tang, along with Li Bai, Du Fu, and Wei Yingwu. How could I not include him? And so I began researching his life.

Liu was born in Chang'an in 773 in the aftermath of the An Lushan Rebellion. Although the city had recovered, the central government had only survived by relying on foreign mercenaries and regional military forces headed by men who paid lip-service but not tax revenues to the court. But at least life in the capital was more or less back to normal.

Both of Liu's parents came from prestigious families whose members had served every Tang emperor. But proximity to the throne could just as easily bring families to ruin. In the case of his, the enthronement of Empress Wu in 690 meant an end to their good fortune. The senior member of the clan had opposed her rise, and once she was empress, she had him killed. The Lius who served thereafter served in the provinces, not at court. Hence, Liu's father was mostly absent, and Zongyuan spent his childhood with his mother's family on a farm outside the capital. It wasn't until he was eleven that he accompanied his father on missions.

Liu then began studying with tutors and attending local academies wherever his father served. Since he was often on his own, he chose his own literary models. Instead of the ornate style preferred by officials, Liu looked to those who had something to say, writers like Zhuangzi and Sima Qian.

When he was sixteen, Liu returned to Chang'an to prepare for the exams required of would-be officials. Due to the dark cloud of Empress Wu, it took five years, but he finally passed. During this time, Liu formed relationships with a number of men serving at court. Not only his literary skills but his reasoning abilities also caught the notice of a reformist group headed by the chief adviser to Li Song, the crown prince.

When Emperor Dezong died at the beginning of 805, Li Song ascended the throne as Shunzong, and began implementing the policies they had discussed—policies meant to curtail, if not end, corruption and usurpation of privilege. They were chiefly aimed at the regional governors and palace eunuchs, and they failed.

Less than four months after becoming emperor, Shunzong was forced to abdicate, and his son became Emperor Xianzong. Besides putting an end to the reforms, Xianzong banished all those who had taken part, which included Liu and seven others. Not only were they banished, they were all demoted to the mere functionary post of assistant magistrate. They would have nothing to do, which was excruciating punishment for men whose lives had been concerned with reforming the government.

The town to which Liu was banished was Yongzhou, at the confluence of the Xiang and Xiao rivers in South China. Not only did his post not include any responsibilities or authority, it didn't even include a place to live. Fortunately, Liu had long been interested in the Dharma, and the abbot of the town's largest monastery welcomed him.

It was an otherwise depressing beginning. Liu's mother and daughter died soon after they arrived. In mourning and without any official responsibilities, Liu began life in exile on what amounted to a forced vacation. He spent his time hiking in the nearby countryside, drinking with like-minded individuals, and writing whatever came to mind. Inspiring him were cousins and friends who joined him. The group that gathered around him became so famous, it was talked about in the capital.

Most periods of exile ended after two years, or five at the most. When the five-year mark passed with no reprieve, Liu concluded he was never going back. He moved out of the monastery and built a house across the Xiao on a small tributary he renamed Stupid River 愚溪 to remind him of his foolhardy attempt at political reform. He didn't take up farming, but he did enjoy the life of a retired gentleman.

Finally, ten years after being exiled, he and the others were recalled. Liu arrived in the capital six weeks later, full of hope. But the hope didn't last long. One of the chancellors was a great-grandson of the Liu-family nemesis, Empress

Wu. Three weeks after they returned, the former assistant magistrates were exiled again. This time they were promoted to serve as magistrates, but their new posts were even farther from the capital. Liu's assignment was to Liuzhou, just north of what is now Vietnam.

If Yongzhou was a provincial backwater, Liuzhou was barely a town. The entire prefecture had a tax-paying population of 7,000, in contrast to Yongzhou's 150,000, and not all those 7,000 spoke Chinese. Liu arrived in a different world. He continued to write, but he finally had work to do, and he devoted himself to carrying it out.

Unfortunately, Liu's health was failing. He suffered from beriberi and constipation, and he contracted cholera. Finally, at the end of 819, he was recalled. But before he could pack, he died. His body was brought back to Chang'an, and he was buried a few villages west of Du Fu's grave. Although I found Du Fu's, I searched in vain for any sign of Liu's.

During the fifteen years Liu spent a thousand miles from home, he produced some of China's greatest literature. His essays became models for later writers, and the ideas he expressed became the staple of thinkers, regardless of their points of view. He even invented a new genre, the hiking journal. But for me, the highlight was his poetry. He didn't leave much, but when it comes to poetry, it doesn't take much. Since I wasn't able to pour any whiskey on his grave, I traveled to where he wrote the poems that follow and stopped long enough to blind some fish in his Stupid River.

from *Written in Exile*

5   Ode for a Caged Eagle

In whistling wind and pelting sleet
an eagle takes off in morning light
flying through clouds cutting through rainbows
it dives like lightning into the hills
slicing through thickets of thorns with its wings
it grabs a rabbit then flies into the sky
other birds scatter from its bloody talons
settling on a perch it surveys its realm
the hot winds of summer suddenly arise
it loses its feathers and goes into hiding
harassed by vermin lurking in the grass
frightened and distressed unable to sleep
all it can think of is the return of cool air
escaping its restraints and soaring into the clouds

[5] Written in Yongzhou most likely in the twelfth month of 805, shortly after Liu arrived at his place of exile. We have no poems about his departure from Chang'an or his journey, but he was accompanied by his mother and a daughter. Although Liu was not imprisoned, his exile came with restrictions. It was a new experience, and the eagle's confinement reminded him of his own predicament. The eagle in this case is one that has been raised from a chick and trained to hunt. Such birds were kept in a pen during the summer molting period while waiting for their flight feathers to grow out again.

7 The First Plum Blossoms

Plum blossoms appear first on the taller trees
shining in the distance against the blue southern sky
the North Wind diffuses their scent at night
heavy frost at dawn adds to their white
I wish I could send them a thousand miles
but with so many mountains and rivers in between
these wintertime flowers would surely fade
how could they console a distant friend

8 Thinking of My Old Garden in Spring

The sound of bureau birds is late
it's time for spring farmwork in Chu
I keep thinking of the water in my old pond
waiting for someone to irrigate the garden

[7] Written in Yongzhou in the first month of 806. The last four lines reprise a poem by Lu Kai (d. 269): "Meeting a courier I broke off a branch / I'm sending it to a friend on the northern border / finding nothing else south of the Yangzi / this branch of spring will have to do."

[8] Written in Yongzhou at the beginning of 806. Liu still expects to return to Chang'an and thinks back to where he grew up near the capital along the Feng River. The term "bureau birds" refers to an ancient division of government into nine bureaus, each named for a bird. Here, in the ancient state of Chu, the local bureaucrats are sleeping late.

9   Meeting a Farmer at the Start of Spring

Spring arrives early in Southern Chu
things start to grow while it's still cold
the power of the earth is loose in the land
hibernating creatures are stirring
there's no color yet in the countryside
but farmers are already plowing
I can hear birds singing in the orchards
I can see springs flowing in the marshes
farming of course is honest work
but an exile is cut off from normal life
my old pond I imagine is overgrown
the family farm all thorns and vines
I admire recluses but I'm not free
nothing I try succeeds
I related all this to a farmer
explaining my situation in detail
he kept rubbing the handle of his plow
and turning to look at the looming clouds

[9] Written in Yongzhou in the spring of 806. Yongzhou was just inside the southern border of the ancient state of Chu. The home Liu refers to was not the one on his father's side just outside the palace in Chang'an, but the farm that belonged to his mother's family southwest of the city between the Feng River and the Shaolin Plateau. This begins like a Tao Yuanming poem, but it doesn't end that way. Instead of expressing a desire to join the farmer, Liu remains a banished official wishing he could return to court.

10 Reading Zen Texts in the Morning at Transcendent Master Temple

Gargling with well water made my teeth chatter
after purifying myself I brushed off my clothes
I happened to pick up a palm-leaf text
leaving the east wing I kept reading
there's nothing to grab in the wellspring of truth
the world keeps chasing footprints of falsehood
I wish I could fathom these ancient words
will I ever be done perfecting my nature
the monastery courtyard is quiet
it's all green moss and bamboo
even sunny days the fog and dew linger
the pine trees look just washed
the peace I feel is hard to describe
I'm happy just being awake

[10] Written in Yongzhou in the summer of 806, when Liu would have been new to a monastic environment. The grounds of Longxing Temple are now home to the city's tax bureau and a primary school. Liu renames the temple here in the abbot's honor. The abbot's name was Chongsun, whom Liu refers to as the "transcendent master." Liu often joined him in his quarters in the temple's east wing to read texts—texts that would have been written on palm leaves in India but on paper or silk in China. Liu's quarters were in the west wing, facing the river.

16 *from* Five Odes to Master Sun's Temple: The Meditation Hall

It begins with the weaving of thatch
surrounding a vacant space
wildflowers falling beyond a darkened door
inside someone without schemes
entering existence without grabbing hold
looking at emptiness without analyzing
ten thousand sounds arise from conditions
deep within there is stillness in noise
the mind and the world are essentially alike
birds leave no tracks when they fly

27 Early Spring in Lingling

Before it departed I asked Spring
when it would reach the Qin Plains
and could it carry a dream back home
all the way to my old garden

[16] Written in Yongzhou in the late summer or early fall of 806. A set of five poems about Longxing Temple included this one about the meditation hall. The abbot was a student of Zen and Tiantai Buddhism, both of which stress meditation.

[27] Written in Yongzhou in the spring of 807. Lingling was another name for Yongzhou. The Qin Plains refer to the area around Chang'an.

31 Drinking Wine

Feeling less than happy this morning
I got up and opened a fresh jug
lifting my cup I thanked the wine gods
for this gift to chase away cares
a moment later I felt different
suddenly the whole world was fine
the gloom disappeared from the mountains
the warmth of the sky filled the river
at the town's overgrown South Rampart
the trees formed a canopy of leaves
the cool shade provided welcome relief
we heard some fine words here last night
once we were drunk and stopped talking
we stretched out on the sweet-smelling grass
the wealthiest men in the past
surely possessed nothing like this

[31] Written in Yongzhou in the summer of 807 shortly after Emperor Xian-zong announced that the "appointments" of the eight men he banished two years earlier, for their involvement in the reform movement, would continue for another three years—so much for returning to court. Yong-zhou's South Rampart overlooked a bend of the Xiao River. It was half a kilometer beyond the town's South Gate and over a kilometer from Liu's residence at Longxing Temple.

32 Transplanting a Hibiscus from the Shore of the Xiang to My Longxing Hermitage

With a loveliness that can't be hidden
how did this lone plant survive
flourishing on the Xiang's west shore
but plagued by wind and dew in fall
this beauty has since left that chilly water
its flowery profusion now graces my veranda
lotuses can hardly compare
up here on higher ground

33 River Snow

A thousand mountains and not a bird flying
ten thousand paths and not a single footprint
an old man in his raincoat in a solitary boat
fishes alone in the freezing river snow

[32] Written in Yongzhou in the summer of 807, or perhaps the following summer, while Liu was living at Longxing Temple. The Xiao River flows through Yongzhou (Lingling) and is joined by the Xiang just north of town. The Xiang, though, is the more famous of the two rivers; hence, Liu often uses its name when referring to the Xiao. The hibiscus can't survive winters north of the Yangzi.

[33] Written in Yongzhou in the winter of 807 when the region experienced a rare and unusually heavy snowfall. The most common foul-weather gear in ancient China was made from the bark of palm trees. This poem became so famous, it was, and still is, a staple of painters.

36 Transplanting a Dozen Cassias from Hengyang to My Hermitage in Lingling

Banished to the southern frontier
passing the sacred peak where the Xiang River winds
I climbed the rush-lined shore at dawn
beneath a cloudless autumn sky
I found some cassias hidden in the weeds
overjoyed I dug them up
from charred ash-covered fields
cleared for firewood long ago
by the road they had gone unnoticed
but the peak is now behind them
their soil was intact when I unpacked them
since the palace on the moon was too far
they were hoping to become home to a phoenix
and they knew what to do when it rained
people in the south admire them now
who would have known but for me
my innermost thoughts I can't share
but it doesn't help keeping them inside

[36] Written in Yongzhou in the fall of 808. Liu dug up these plants near Hengyang—and its nearby sacred peak of Hengshan—on his way into exile in the winter of 805. Once he arrived, he wasn't allowed to travel outside the Yongzhou area. Here they are nearly three years later. The cassia is identified with transcendence and is said to grow on the moon—and Liu identifies with the cassia. The phoenix only appears when a benevolent ruler is on the throne. Normally a phoenix will only alight on a paulownia, but Liu hopes, should one appear, it will make an exception.

37　At Night in Early Autumn, for Wu Wuling

Gusts of mist blow through the bamboo
magpies flutter in the bushes
my friend is on the Xiang's far shore
and the autumn wind lasts all night
the fog is too thick to see through
and the cresting waves never end
I can't say the one I miss is far
but I'm not with him tonight
a lover of uncommon music
he strings his paulownia with red silk
echoing in the Western Vault
his notes surge across the sky
spontaneous not contrived
the work of Heaven not effort
simplicity hidden in the subtlest of sounds
something a deaf fool wouldn't understand

[37] Written in Yongzhou in the fall of 808. Wu Wuling (d. 834) was banished
to Yongzhou earlier that year and quickly became one of Liu's most fre-
quent companions. Wu settled on the west shore of the Xiao (here referred
to as the Xiang), across from Liu's residence at Longxing Temple. When
Wu returned to the capital in 812, he asked Chancellor Pei Du to pardon
Liu, but to no avail. Both Liu and Wu were adept at playing the zither.
For such instruments, paulownia wood was prized for its lightness as well
as its sound. Until modern times, zithers were strung with silk thread, as
the music was intended for friends, not neighbors. The forces of autumn
are said to rise from the Western Vault of Heaven.

41   Feeling Decrepit

I knew old age would find me
I never guessed I would watch it arrive
I shouldn't be decrepit so young
but I'm beginning to see the signs
like gaps in my teeth and thinning hair
and not enough stamina to run
but what good does complaining do
at least my mind remains unaffected
and where are Pengzu or Laozi
the Duke of Zhou or Confucius
the ones we call centenarians or sages
none of them is alive today
all I want is good wine
and a few friends to share it
spring is nearly over
the fruit trees have leafed out
the sun is shining and the sky is pure blue
hearing a migrating swan in the distance
I walked out my door and yelled to my friends
grab your canes we're off to the woods
let's have some fun and try singing
those ancient lines from the Odes of Shang

[41] Written in Yongzhou in the late spring of 809. At the end, Liu yells to
his friends and fellow exiles also staying at the monastery. These odes were
chanted with drums and gongs and little concern for their meaning.

51   Planting a Lingshou Tree

Seeing my white hair in an icy stream
I was relieved to be in the countryside
walking along I asked an old man
who repeated this delightful name
since becoming lame and decrepit
and quitting work in my prime
not waiting for the gift of a cane
I decided to transplant one of these
while my garden flowers were showing off
it opened its buds outside my room
its drooping stem soon straightened
it grew stronger and multiplied
when I use one of these my feet don't feel tired
my steps have begun to feel lighter
and it doesn't need to be shortened
it's the perfect thing for a hike

[51] Written in Yongzhou in the winter of 809 while living at Longxing Monastery. Lingshou produces multiple, jointed, bamboo-like stems about eight feet long and three to four inches around. An empress once gave one to her senior adviser. In exile, Liu saw no sense in waiting for such a present. Lingshou's "delightful name," in Chinese 靈壽木, means "plant of long life."

56   After a Rain Taking a Morning Walk Alone
to the Pond North of the Yuxi

Sandbars free of overnight clouds
village walls lit by the morning sun
a pristine pond encircled by trees
last night's rain scattered by the wind
happy having nothing to do
my mind becomes one with all this

58   Inspecting the Yuxi after an Early Summer Rain

After a long rain the sky finally cleared
I followed the river's winding shore
testing weed-covered springs with my staff
tying back young bamboo with my sash
why do I mutter so much
I want to be alone I guess
thanks to my freedom from running errands
I can sing or keep still when it's hot

[56] Written in Yongzhou in the summer of 810. Liu finally moved out of the
monastery and built a house across the Xiao on a side stream he called the
Yuxi 愚溪 (Stupid River), his reasoning being: it was due to his stupidity
that he ended up there. The pond was just north of his house.

[58] Written in Yongzhou in the summer of 810. Liu's post as deputy magis-
trate came with no real duties—hence his residence on a minor tributary
across the river from the town where he was "serving."

59   Riverside Home

I had grown tired of court attire
this rustication among hill tribes was welcome
with nothing to do and farmers for neighbors
sometimes I feel like a recluse
at dawn tilling dew-covered grass
at dusk banging oars on river rocks
not meeting anyone coming or going
I sing out loud beneath the blue southern sky

62   Getting Up at Midnight to Gaze at My West Garden

Awakened by the sound of dripping dew
I opened the door to my west garden
the winter moon was rising from East Ridge
turning the bamboo pale white
the waterfall upstream sounded louder
now and then I heard a bird cry
I leaned against a pillar until dawn
wondering how to put such solitude into words

[59] Written in Yongzhou in the fall of 810. Although Han Chinese made up the majority of the population, the more mountainous parts of this region were home to a number of ethnic minorities. The Yuxi was narrow in places and lined with boulders—hence "banging oars on river rocks."

[62] Written in the winter of 810. East Ridge refers to the ridges behind the monastery where Liu lived his first five years in Yongzhou. The Yuxi included a number of cascades upstream from Liu's new residence.

63 Living out of Town at the End of the Year

Living in seclusion near a mountain village
I'm surprised to be on my own at year-end
a woodcutter's song drifts in from the wilds
ashes from a fire settle in my yard
worldly distractions have become more distant
pleasures too have waned with the year
I consider in silence why this is so
but why compare the present with the past

65 Walking to the Ferry after a Rain

When the rain finally stopped I decided to stretch my legs
I headed for the ferry before the sun could set
as the water level dropped the ferry path appeared
hanging in the trees was storm debris

[63] Written in Yongzhou in the winter of 810. The end of one year and beginning of another is when friends and relatives visit each other and celebrate their longevity. Most of Liu's friends were on the east shore. An uncle who also lived on the west shore died earlier that year, and a cousin left the previous year. Also, this was Liu's first winter on his own. He spent the previous five at Longxing Monastery.

[65] Written in the summer of 811. One of the ferries that connected the east and west banks of the Xiao did so at the mouth of the Yuxi River, several hundred meters downstream from where Liu was living. The precipitous drop in the water level was along the Yuxi, not the Xiao.

66 Passing through a Deserted Village on an Autumn Morning Walk to South Valley

At the end of autumn after a heavy frost
I set off early for a secluded valley
the bridge was covered with yellow leaves
nothing remained of the village but old trees
except for a few hardy flowers it was bleak
overgrown springs gurgled faintly
having given up schemes long ago
I wonder why I frightened the deer

68 Occasional Poem on a Summer Day

Here in the south it's so hot I feel drunk
after dozing on a bench I opened the north window
it was noon and I couldn't hear any other sound
just a farm boy pounding tea beyond the bamboo

[66] Written in Yongzhou in the late fall of 811. South Valley was two kilometers south of his Yuxi hermitage.

[68] Written in the summer of 812. During the Tang, tea leaves were often processed by pounding them in a mortar after they had been oxidized by heat. The resulting powder was then whisked with boiling water and drunk.

75 Presented to Chief Minister Li and Assistant Censor Yuan in Lingling, Also Sent to Wu Wuling

A well-ordered world disdains officials
hence our rustication to the Xiang
with sunlight filling the four quarters
who needs someone to strike a flint
perching on snags with battered wings
we warble our sad songs to each other
clouds from the north bring a frigid wind
the end of autumn and desolate days
gentlemen prefer to acquiesce
lesser men would rather quarrel
seeing how miserable we look every day
and the sorrow of separation increasing
let's empty this jug of wine
and indulge ourselves in song
too bad no musicians are present
to do these poems of ours justice

[75] Written in Yongzhou (Lingling) in the late fall of 812 and addressed to Liu's fellow exiles Li Youqing and Yuan Keji. Liu uses the titles of the offices they held prior to their exile. The poem is also addressed to Wu Wuling, who was exiled to Yongzhou in 808, but who was pardoned in the summer of 812 and had since returned to the capital.

76 Invited to Accompany Magistrate Wei to the Huang River to Pray for Rain: An Impromptu Poem upon Reaching the Shrine

The summer sun exceeded what farmers could bear
our noble lord was worried about the crops
we rode beneath a crescent moon with his aides
their whistles echoed across a sapphire sky
we followed a woodcutter's path to its end
we finally stopped near a rustic dwelling
by a pure cold stream at the mouth of a valley
among ancient trees at a forest shrine
in a damp autumn fog we lit incense
in the first rays of dawn we offered wine
the buzzing flies of a shaman's drone
ritual objects perfectly arranged
an auspicious breeze flattened the grass
surely a welcome rain will follow
a sham official waiting to be punished
I offer these words utterly embarrassed

[76] Written in Yongzhou in the fifth month of 813. The magistrate of Yongzhou at the time was Wei Biao. Liu was the town's deputy magistrate—a post without duties—and he finds himself embarrassed to take part in an official ceremony. Reed whistles were used to clear a path or announce the approach of an official. The source of the Huang River was thirty-five kilometers east of Yongzhou. Liu also describes the scenic highlights of this occasion in one of his travel journals.

77 Hearing a Gibbon on the Huang River

The riverside path winds for miles
where is that gibbon howling
this banished official has no more tears
its heartbreaking cries are in vain

84 Recalled to the Capital, I Send This to Friends Back in Lingling

I keep thinking about this minnow in that tiny pond
then worry about these puny wings trying to reach Heaven
I've lost count of the markers along the shore
each one farther from where we parted

[77] Written in Yongzhou in the fifth month of 813. The terms of Liu's exile did not normally allow him to go so far afield, but since he was asked to accompany the magistrate, this was a rare opportunity for him to indulge his love of exploration.

[84] Written in the middle of the first month of 815 on his way back to Chang'an. Lingling was an old name for Yongzhou. Liu thinks about the decade he has spent there and his impending return to the empyrean heights at court. Major roads and waterways in China were lined with distance markers every five *li* (two and a half kilometers).

89 On My Way Back, I Climbed the Plateau North of Hanyang and Wrote This at the Linchuan Post Station

As I hurried toward palace gates
I stopped to look around Linchuan
I wasn't embarrassed by the rubble
I was saddened nothing had been done
a few pines marked where there used to be a temple
traces of snow where there once were terraced fields
the scenes of village life were depressing
after so many years the place still looked hopeless

95 Reaching the Ba River Pavilion in the Second Month after Being Summoned Back to the Capital

Eleven years ago I was a southbound exile
four thousand *li* later I'm in the north again
together with the summons warm weather arrived too
along the postal route new flowers every day

[89] Written at the end of the first month of 815 at a postal station near Hanyang. Liu stayed here with his father in 783. In 781, imperial armies put down a rebellion in this region, and Liu returns to see the place still hasn't recovered.

[95] Written in the second half of the second month of 815. The Ba River Pavilion was just east of the capital and was where people often welcomed or said goodbye to friends. The distance from Yongzhou to the capital via Hanyang was 2,000 *li* (1,000 kilometers) each way.

97 On the Xiang Again

Hello waters of the Xiang
I'm back on you again today
who knows once I leave you
when I'll return from yet another exile

100 Parting from Mengde Again

We've followed the same path the past twenty years
suddenly this morning we're taking separate roads
if imperial grace should permit us to return
let's spend our last years living next to farmers

[97] After less than a month in the capital, Liu was exiled again. This poem was written in the middle of the fourth month of 815. After crossing the Yangzi and Dongting Lake, Liu continued his journey up the Xiang to his new place of exile, another three hundred kilometers past Yongzhou.

[100] Written in Hengyang near the end of the fourth month of 815 on Liu's way to his new place of exile. Liu Yuxi (Mengde) and Liu Zongyuan knew each other as students, passed the civil service exam the same year (793), and served in several posts together until both were exiled in 805. All they can hope for now is "imperial grace" and a future limited to farming rather than serving at court. Liu couldn't get Tao Yuanming out of his mind.

104 Traveling by River in Lingnan

Sailing south on infested waters into a land of mist
horizon of tanglehead stretching to the sea
hills marked by elephant swaths after a rain
dragon drool rising from the depths in the sun
poison-spitting frogs that can see a traveler's shadow
a typhoon sky frightening the passengers on board
my concerns however are other than these
namely how to bear white hair and the disappearing years

105 Sent to Family and Friends via a Fellow Bronze Fish Official on His Way to the Capital

After traveling over mountains thousands of miles
I arrived to find this settlement deserted
such districts only get bronze fish officials
I won't be sending any more long-distance letters

[104] Liu wrote this in the sixth month of 815. His route took him up the Xiang, into the Li River via the locks of the Lingchu Canal, then south on the Li, and finally west, up the Xun and the Liujiang, to his place of exile. Lingnan refers to the provinces bordering Vietnam. "Dragon drool" is river vapor. The region was also known for a frog that spit sand at a person's shadow. Typhoons are often preceded by unusually clear skies.

[105] Written in Liuzhou a few weeks later. This official was another magistrate and carried a bronze fish as an emblem of office. Such officials were allowed to send only government-related correspondence with the regular courier service. Personal letters depended on friends.

106 Climbing Liuchou Tower—Sent to the Magistrates of Zhang, Ding, Feng, and Lian Counties

The city tower here borders the wilderness
my cares are as endless as the ocean sky
a sudden wind churns the lotus-filled water
a downpour beats against the vine-covered wall
ridgetop trees block distant views
the river's bends are as tortuous as my thoughts
since coming to this land of tattooed tribes
we share a realm beyond the reach of letters

108 The Hill Tribes of Liuzhou

People south of town have to ford the river
with different clothes and speech they're hard to get to know
they wrap salt in bamboo leaves to take back to the hills
and roll up rice in lily pads to eat on market days
they make goose-feather quilts to protect against the cold
prognosticate with chicken bones and worship water spirits
at court it's such a bother talking through interpreters
I'd like to toss my hat away and get a few tattoos

[106] Written in the early fall of 815. The four friends in the title were also exiled a second time for their involvement in the reform movement.

[108] Written in the fall of 815. Han Chinese are still in the minority in the Liuzhou region. Officials were required to wear a hat in public.

118 Presented in the Rain to Hermit Jia of Immortal Peak

Last night a winter rain poured on the river
this morning the clouds hid Immortal Peak
I'm guessing that panther is up there somewhere
laughing at you stuck down here in the mud

121 Impromptu Poem on the Falling of Banyan Leaves in the Second Month in Liuzhou

As a failure and a stranger I'm equally depressed
with spring resembling fall I'm also confused
when it rains in this hill town all the flowers disappear
banyan leaves cover the ground and orioles keep singing

[118] Written in Liuzhou in the winter of 815. The Daoist hermit Jia Peng lived on Immortal Peak, directly across the Liujiang River from Liuzhou. Apparently, he decided to spend some time in town, but the trail back up the mountain was too steep (and slick) to attempt in the rain.

[121] Written in Liuzhou in the spring of 816. Rains here are not as gentle as they are in Yongzhou. Also, banyans in this part of China lose their leaves in spring, not in autumn. Liu, though not the orioles, has a hard time accepting this.

139 Waking Up Alone

The windows were fogged when I awoke
it was a pitter-patter rainy morning
I hate setting off on a good hike late
but I was overwhelmed by minor tasks
you ask what I think about statecraft
who among the ancients understood it

140 Joking about Planting Willows

Magistrate Willow of Willow Town
planted willows beside Willow River
such a play on words might become a story
perhaps one set in the past
with hanging branches shading the ground
and soaring trunks touching the sky
such trees might remind people of me
but alas of no wisdom that improved their lives

[139] Liu didn't have any responsibilities in Yongzhou, but he did in Liuzhou—hence the "minor tasks" and thoughts about "statecraft." Six-line poems were rare in the Tang, but Liu left us three.

[140] Written in Liuzhou at the beginning of 819. The play on words here involved Liu's surname and the name of the town and its river, all of which share the same character 柳. His ur-ancestor, Zhan Huo, sat under a willow and dispensed advice, and people started calling him the Wise Man Under the Willow. This marked the beginning of the Liu clan to which Liu Zongyuan belonged, a member of its fortieth generation.

QU YUAN

Qu Yuan 屈原

Before the Three Gorges Dam raised the level of the Yangzi one hundred and fifty meters, there was a small town in the middle of the gorges that clung to the north shore. It was called Zigui 秭歸. One day thirty years ago, I got off a boat that ferried passengers up and down the river, and from Zigui I took the daily bus that followed the Xiangxi River upstream to Xingshan. A dozen kilometers later, I got off where there was a suspension bridge and hiked into a gorge on the other side. Half an hour later, I came out in the mountain-ringed farming valley of Lepingli 樂平里. At about the time Aristotle was tutoring Alexander the Great, Qu Yuan was born here in 340 BCE.

Despite the passage of time, there were a few things the villagers of Lepingli still connected to Qu Yuan. The cave he used as his study was still there, as was the hillside well whose water he used to wash the dust of the world from his eyes. Also still there was the shrine hall built where the family house once stood. Inside, the walls were lined with stone tablets on which all of Qu Yuan's poems were carved—paid for with the savings of a village teacher who served a twenty-year sentence for promoting Rightist Thought. There was something else, though not on display: the tattered volumes of poems written in Qu Yuan's honor by the farmers of Lepingli over the past six hundred years. They're the pride of the world's second oldest poetry club, second only to l'Académie des Jeux floraux, founded a century earlier in Toulouse to honor poets who wrote in Occitan, rather than French.

Oddly, the man venerated by the poet-farmers of Lepingli, as well as by Chinese everywhere, is an enigma. Of course there are stories, but few that aren't made up. I would have liked to know, for example, how a boy from Lepingli rose to become one of the two deputy prime ministers, namely, Minister of the Left, as well as Lord of the Three Gates of what was the most powerful state of the Middle Kingdom at the time.

The first position empowered Qu Yuan to advise his king on policies regarding neighboring states, and the second gave him control over the religious affairs of Chu's three most powerful clans, which included the education of their sons. Not surprisingly, in the dozens of poems attributed to him, Qu Yuan never tires of urging his king to follow the wisdom of the sages and of seeking to transmit such wisdom to others. He was a shaman and a teacher who trained whole hillsides of young men in the virtues and ways of the sages.

Although we know next to nothing about Qu Yuan's time at court, he was said to have been self-assured and unafraid of speaking his mind. But forthright people rarely last long where power is involved. Qu Yuan aroused the jealousy and envy of others and eventually their slander. When the king believed the slander, Qu Yuan was banished beyond the Han River to the northern border of Chu. His king, meanwhile, ignored Qu Yuan's advice to beware the state of Qin and died a few years later as its prisoner.

Qu Yuan was later recalled to court, but the king's son and successor was not receptive and banished him once more, this time to the south, beyond the Yangzi, to the region surrounding Dongting Lake. A dozen years later, in 278 BC, Qu Yuan heard that Chu's capital had been sacked by the Qin army. Feeling that his world had ended, he walked into the Miluo River carrying a large stone, not far from where the river enters the lake, and drowned.

On the fifth day of the fifth lunar month, Chinese everywhere commemorate Qu Yuan's death by rowing boats on rivers and lakes, hoping to reach his body before the water dragons do, and by making rice tamales to throw into the water as a distraction—or to eat with friends and loved ones. In his honor, the day is celebrated in China as Poet's Day.

Before Qu Yuan, poems in the Middle Kingdom read as if they could have been written by anyone. China's earliest anthology of poetry, the *Shijing,* included over three hundred poems but not the name of a single poet. Qu Yuan changed this. It was his voice. He was a poet. Wang Wei once said he never traveled anywhere without taking two books with him: the *Vimalakirti Sutra,* from which he took his own pen name, and the poems of Qu Yuan. He wasn't alone. It's hard to find any Chinese poet of the past whose verse wasn't affected, if not inspired, by what Qu Yuan wrote and by the way he wrote.

I read his poetry for the first time in 1977, not long after I moved from Haiming Monastery to the farming village of Bamboo Lake. After working my way through the sutras, reading Qu Yuan's "Beset by Sorrow"—at least the parts I understood—was like flying. It reminded me of the feeling I'd had when I first read Hart Crane's *The Bridge*. If you're up for it, summon the wind. With the Kunlun Mountains within reach, why not see for yourself what the immortals are up to?

from *A Shaman's Lament:* Beset by Sorrow

Scion of Emperor Gaoyang   1
offspring of the noble Boyong
when the new year's stars were high
on the twenty-seventh day I descended.
After studying the time of my appearance   5
my father gave me an auspicious name
he called me Realized Exemplar
Impartial Spirit for my sobriquet.
Blessed with an abundance of inner beauty
to which I added arts and skills   10
I wore angelica and lovage
sewed autumn orchids into my sash.
I hurried as if I were late
worried this wasn't my time
I gathered gardenias in the hills in the morning   15
evenings I picked slough grass on sandbars.
The months and years wouldn't wait
springs and autumns kept trading places
seeing plants and trees stripped bare

---

[1] Emperor Shun (r. 2255–2205 BCE), whose grave Qu Yuan visits later.
[3] The stars of Boötes, which include Arcturus.
[11] *Angelica dahurica* and *Ligusticum striatum*.
[12] Officials wore sashes to which they also attached their seals of office.
[16] *Beckmannia syzigachne.*

I feared my fair one's time was short.   20
Not nurturing new growth or getting rid of weeds
why doesn't he change his ways
mount a winged steed and ride forth
join me on the road of the ancients?
The purity of the Three Lords of old   25
was ensured by the presence of fragrant plants
they didn't just twine cymbidium and angelica
they mixed cinnamon bark and pepper.
The greatness and glory of Yao and Shun
came from following the Way   30
Jie and Zhou chose unrestraint
taking shortcuts they became lost.
I think of court favorites indulging in pleasures
their paths unlit and lined with danger
it isn't the loss of my own life I fear   35
but the rout of my liege's chariots.
I hurried before and behind him
on the tracks of the former kings

[20] Referring to his ruler, King Huai (r. 328–299 BCE).

[25] Yao, Shun, and Yu the Great laid the basis for the Xia dynasty (2205–1766 BCE), from which the ruling clans of Chu traced their descent.

[27] Cymbidiums are commonly referred to as "boat orchids."

[28] Sichuan pepper, not the black variety native to India.

[31] The last kings of the Xia and Shang dynasties, respectively.

[36] In 316 BCE, the state of Qin invaded and occupied the area west of the Yangzi Gorges and began a series of incursions into Chu in the north.

but sweet flag saw not my heart
deceived by slander he spurned me.   40
Of course I knew the perils of being forthright
but I couldn't stop and persisted
I pointed to the heavens as my guide
all for the sake of my lord.
He welcomed my counsel at first   45
then changing his mind he turned to others
it wasn't the estrangement that troubled me
but my august one's vacillation.
I cultivated whole hillsides of orchids
slopes of cymbidiums too   50
fields of peonies and goosenecks
meadows of asarum and angelica.
I hoped at the peak of their growth
I could harvest them if I were patient
seeing them wither wasn't what hurt   55
but such sweet plants turn into weeds.
People compete out of avarice and greed
they never have enough and want more
their hearts aroused by jealousy and envy
they criticize others but forgive themselves.   60

[39] Throughout this poem *Acorus calamus* (sweet flag) refers to King Huai.

[40] Qu Yuan was exiled by King Huai and by his son, King Qingxiang.

[51] *Paeonia albiflora* and *Lysimachia clethroides.*

[56] The implication is that the "plants" refer to his protégés—the sons of the nobility under his tutelage as Lord of the Three Gates.

Suddenly they're off chasing something else
but not what concerns my heart
the steady advance of old age
the failure to leave a better name.
I sip magnolia dew in the morning   65
dine on chrysanthemum petals at night
as long as my waist reflects my inner beauty
what harm is a sallow complexion.
I use tree roots to wrap angelica
thread fallen fig flower stamens   70
twine cinnamon bark and cymbidiums
tie snow parsley so that it dangles.
I take my patterns from practitioners of the past
not from what the world wears
though not popular with people today   75
the ways of Peng and Xian are my guide.
I wipe my tears and can't help sigh
lamenting the hardships of worldly life
despite my restraint in the cultivation of beauty
I'm disparaged in the morning and dismissed at night.   80
But whenever they dismiss my cymbidium sash

---

[67] Inner beauty—represented by the sachets on his sash—is at the core of
Qu Yuan's persona: half mortal, half spirit.

[72] *Cnidium monnieri.*

[76] Peng and Xian were two legendary shamans associated with the origins
of medicine and divination, respectively.

[78] Qu Yuan is speaking as the spirit Realized Exemplar.

I add angelica to make it longer
such things truly gladden my heart
I could die a dozen deaths and still have no regrets.
I only hate how my dear one dallies   85
how he never considers people's hearts
how his ladies envy my eyebrows
how they gossip and say I'm licentious.
People today are so clever
realigning their compass and square   90
disdaining plumb lines in favor of curves
their standard trying to please.
Worried anxious and depressed
I alone am bereft in this age
I wish I could suddenly die and disappear   95
I can't bear to go on this way.
A falcon doesn't mix with other birds
at least that was true in the past
how can a circle and square match
or those with different views live in peace.   100
Humbling themselves and their aspirations
enduring insults and blame
concealing their purity and dying for what is right
this is what the ancients revered.
Regretful I hadn't seen where the road led   105
I stopped and changed directions
I turned my carriage around and went back
I hadn't gone too far astray.
I walked my horse through an orchid-filled marsh

raced up a hill of pepper and rested   110
unable to go farther without incurring blame
I went home and refashioned my attire.
I wove lotus leaves into a jacket
their petals into a skirt
I'm done with those who don't know me   115
as long as my heart's fragrance stays true.
May my hat be as high as a mountain
and my flower-decked sash wind forever
whether mingling among the sweet or the rank
may its radiance remain undimmed.   120
Suddenly looking back I let my eyes roam
I gazed on the wilds all around me
my sash adorned with sachets
the fragrance was stronger than ever.
Everyone finds joy in something   125
my constant is a love of beauty
even dismembered I wouldn't change
how could I forsake my heart?
My sisters though were distraught
they beseeched me again and again   130

---

[114] Men and women wore robes of different kinds, but men also wore jackets as well as skirts with leggings underneath.

[117] The headgear of officials was usually made of starched silk and rarely of modest height.

[129] The Chinese *nu-xu* 女媭 means one or more "sisters." Most shamans in Chu were female.

Gun was steadfast but heedless
he ended up dying in the wilds of Yu.
Why go on about your love of beauty
how you alone possess such refinement
our house is filled with cockleburs and ferns   135
yet you alone refuse to wear them.
You can't go talking to all those you meet
asking them to examine your heart
people want friends and allies
why remain aloof and not listen?   140
With the sages of the past as my guides
I could only sigh and endure this
I traveled south across the Yuan and the Xiang
before Chonghua I voiced my lament.

[132] Shun tasked Gun with stopping the flooding of the Yellow River. When he failed, he was executed on Mount Yu. Gun's son, Yu the Great, succeeded and later founded the Xia dynasty in 2205 BCE.

[135] The reference to a "house" suggests a shaman coven or guild.

[143] The waters of the Yuan and Xiang drain into Dongting Lake.

[144] After listening to his fellow shamans (or sisters) advocate compromise, Qu Yuan seeks instruction—which for shamans usually came in the form of a vision. Here he visits the grave of his ancestor, Emperor Shun. Chonghua was Shun's name before becoming emperor. He was later referred to by his title, Gaoyang. The grave was six hundred kilometers south of the Chu capital and near the source of the Xiao River and would have required a journey (mostly by boat) of several weeks.

Despite Qi's Nine Songs and Nine Declarations 145
Tai Kang sought nothing but pleasure
oblivious of trouble he made no plans
his five sons lost their homes and their lands.
Wanton Lord Yi never tired of hunting
he loved to shoot borderland foxes 150
such dissipation seldom ends well
Zhuo had designs on his wife.
Jiao was fond of displaying his might
he couldn't stop indulging his desires
he forgot himself in ceaseless pleasure 155
until the day he lost his head.
Jie's course was equally perverse
he likewise met with disaster
neither did the Shang line last

[145] Qi inherited the Xia throne from his father, Yu the Great, and is said to have composed the Nine Songs and the Nine Declarations extolling the virtue of his father. Qi's son, Tai Kang, ignored such lessons.

[149] Hou Yi usurped the Xia throne from Tai Kang. However, archery, not governing, was his real passion, and no border was safe from his expeditions. Zhuo was his chief minister and incited Yi's family to kill him, then claimed Yi's wife for his own and usurped the throne.

[153] Jiao was the son of Zhuo. His mother was Hou Yi's former wife. After killing Zhuo, he was killed by Shao Kang, who restored the Xia dynasty.

[157] Jie was known for his tyranny. He was the last ruler of the Xia dynasty.

Lord Xin was minced and pickled.   160
Tang and Yu were stern and respectful
the Zhou kings never strayed from the Way
promoting the worthy and employing the able
they adhered to the carpenter's line.
Heaven above has no favorites   165
it assists where it finds men of virtue
only where the wisdom of sages thrives
does someone obtain this land below.
I've considered the former and latter
and the principles of these men   170
how someone unjust could be employed
how someone unfit could serve.
Finding myself approaching the end
looking back I have no regrets
making the shaft before measuring the hole   175
virtuous men were often steeped in brine.

---

[160] The Xia was followed by the Shang dynasty (1766–1123 BCE). Lord Xin was its last king. Throughout his poem, Qu Yuan's historical focus is on the Xia, as his clan and most of the other clans at the Chu court traced their descent through its kings.

[161] Yu the Great and Cheng Tang founded the Xia and Shang dynasties, respectively. The Shang was followed by the Zhou (1122–255 BCE).

[168] Those who followed the Way founded dynasties, those who didn't caused their destruction.

[175] Qu Yuan sees himself as a shaft carved according to measurements of the past in search of a matching hole. But standards, alas, have changed.

[176] This completes Qu Yuan's lament to Shun.

I felt so depressed I sobbed
at odds alas with my time
with cymbidium petals I wiped the tears
that soaked my robe's lapels.   180
As I knelt on the hem and expressed my lament
this inner realization blazed forth
I mounted a great bird and four-dragon team
amid dust and wind I suddenly set off.
My carriage left Cangwu at dawn   185
I reached the Hanging Gardens by dusk
I wanted to linger at Spirit Gate
but the light was beginning to fade.
I told the sun's driver to pull back on her reins
to slow down so I could gaze on Sunset Peak   190
the road ahead was long and hard
and I wanted to experience it all.
I watered my horses at Sunrise Lake
then tied the reins to the Fusang Tree

[183] Qu Yuan climbs aboard a carriage resembling a great bird pulled by a team of horses he likens to dragons. This is, of course, a vision.

[185] The name of the area where Emperor Shun's grave was located.

[186] These gardens were at the summit of the Kunlun Mountains, 3,000 kilometers northwest of Shun's grave. Beyond the gardens was Spirit Gate, and beyond that the celestial Land of Immortals.

[189] Xi He and her team of horses pull the sun across the sky.

[190] The sun was said to enter the earth behind Sunset Peak (Mount Yanzi), thirty kilometers south of Tianshui in Gansu province.

[193] The sun enjoys a daily morning bath in Xianchi Lake.

after brushing the sun with its branches   195
I wandered awhile for pleasure.
I instructed the moon's driver to ride ahead
the god of the wind to follow behind
phoenixes cleared the path
but Lei Gong said I wasn't ready.   200
I ordered the phoenixes to fly higher
and to keep flying day and night
whirlwinds gathered to greet me
welcoming me with clouds and rainbows.
Amid ceaseless comings and goings   205
bewildering patterns overhead and below
I told the chamberlain to open the gate
but he stood at the threshold and stared.
The day was late and about to end
I knotted wild orchids while waiting   210
the world can't see past its own corruption
it covers up beauty out of envy.

---

[195] After rising from its bath behind the Fusang Tree, the sun is brushed off, according to the *Shuowen Jiezi,* with the tree's branches.

[197] The goddess whose horses pull the moon across the sky is Wang Shu. The god of the wind is Fei Lian: part deer, part bird.

[200] Lei Gong is also in charge of judging people. Presumably Qu Yuan's status as a mortal disqualifies him from entering the Land of Immortals.

[201] Ignoring the thunder god's declaration, Qu Yuan tells the phoenixes to find another path to Spirit Gate.

[208] As the shaman Realized Exemplar, Qu Yuan is able to embark on a spirit journey, but he is still a mortal and cannot enter the spirit realm.

Before crossing the White River the next morning
I tethered my mounts then climbed Langfeng
as I looked around my tears began to fall   215
the summit was barren of women.
Then suddenly I was visiting the Palace of Spring
I broke off a jade branch to add to my sash
since it hadn't yet lost its blossoms
I could give it to someone below.   220
I told the god of weather to ride the clouds
to find Lady Fu's location
removing a sachet from my sash as a token
I told Jian Xiu to present my case.

[213] Anyone who drinks the water of this river is said to live forever. From the Kunlun Mountains it flows north then disappears into the Taklamakan Desert.

[214] Qu Yuan has not given up. Finding another route, he ascends again, but this time on his own. Langfeng is that part of the summit where the Hanging Gardens and Spirit Gate are located. Although he hopes to join the immortals, Qu Yuan's quest is all too human—and the Land of Immortals not all he hoped it would be.

[217] Qu Yuan's quest suddenly changes from entering the spirit realm to finding a mate—even a semi-immortal one will do. The Palace of Spring was the residence of the legendary emperor Fu Xi.

[221] The god of clouds and weather was Feng Zhong.

[222] Lady Fu was Fu Xi's daughter. She was married to the god of the Yellow River but was abducted by Hou Yi and became his consort.

[224] Jian Xiu means "lame beauty" and refers to Nu Wa, who had no legs, her lower half being that of a serpent. She was the wife of Fu Xi and also the patroness of marriage.

Despite a flurry of comings and goings 225
Lady Fu turned stubborn and unreceptive
in the evening she returned to Qiongshi Rock
in the morning she washed her hair at Weipan Pool.
Guarding her beauty with aloof disdain
she spent her time in idle pleasure 230
despite her allure she lacked propriety
off I went to search elsewhere.
I scanned the four directions
then circled the heavens and descended
in the distance atop Jade Tower 235
I saw the cloistered daughters of Yousong.
I asked a snake-bird to be my go-between
but she said it wouldn't work
a pigeon offered to try
but I didn't like his devious ways. 240
I felt hesitant and suspicious

227 Qiongshi Rock was where Hou Yi lived. It was south of Luoyang near the source of the Luo River. Wang Yi says Weipan Pool was near the source of the Wei River eight hundred kilometers to the west.

231 Commentators attribute Lady Fu's "lack of propriety" to her assent to becoming Hou Yi's consort—as if she had a choice.

235 A ruler of the legendary state of Yousong built a tower in which he housed his daughters until he could find suitable mates.

237 This mythical bird, known as a *zhen*, ate snakes, and its feathers were said to be poisonous.

239 The Chinese consider pigeons the stupidest of birds, as they don't know how to make nests and use those made by other birds instead.

I would have gone myself but that wasn't allowed
finally a phoenix took my gift
but I feared Gao Xin would get there first.
Despite its efforts the bird found no perch   245
all it could do was fly idly around
at least they hadn't married Shao Kang
he was still with Yusi's daughters.
My suit was weak and my go-between clumsy
and I feared my instructions weren't clear   250
corrupt and jealous of the worthy
the world conceals beauty and extols what I hate.
With his inner chamber beyond my reach
and the wise king no longer awake
and me not able to express my feelings   255
how could I stay any longer?
I requested bindweed and divination slips

[244] Gao Xin was the name of Emperor Ku of the third millennium BCE.
One of his wives was one of the Yousong girls, Jiandi, who gave birth to
the founder of the lineage that established the Shang dynasty. Obviously,
Gao Xin did get there before Qu Yuan. However, during a spirit quest, as
in a dream, time is an ocean, not a river. Qu Yuan sees the Yousong girls
while they were still unwed.

[248] Yusi was the grandson of Emperor Shun, Qu Yuan's own ancestor. Shao
Kang married Yusi's two daughters prior to restoring the Xia.

[253] His spirit quest ended, Qu Yuan finds himself back at the grave of
Emperor Shun. His comments, of course, are also meant for his own ruler,
who is likewise beyond his reach and unawake.

[257] The twisted stems of bindweed (*Calystegia*) were used in Chu for divina-

then I asked the oracle their meaning.
She said *Two beauties are a certain match*
but who admires true beauty?
The Nine Kingdoms might be the greatest of realms
but not the only place with maidens
don't be afraid of a distant journey
what seeker of beauty could refuse you?
What land doesn't have fragrant plants
why be attached to your old home
the people of this world are blinded by delusions
why ask them to examine your faults and strengths?
What others love and hate isn't the same
except for those hangers-on at court
filling their waistbands with mugwort
saying wild orchids aren't fit to wear.
Unable to tell one plant from another
how could they appreciate beauty
stuffing their sachets with dung
claiming pepper has no scent?
I hoped I could follow the oracle's words
but I felt anxious and doubtful

260

265

270

275

tion but exactly how is not recorded. Divination also included choosing
among bamboo slips on which fortunes were written.

[258] The grave of Emperor Shun would have included a shrine with priests
and shamans in residence.

[261] China of the first millennium BCE consisted of nine major kingdoms.

[271] *Artemisia argyi.*

since Xian would be descending that night
I prepared offerings of peppered rice.   280
Hundreds of deities came fluttering down
welcomed by the guardians of Jiuyi Mountain
as the spirit's light blazed bright
she explained why my fortune was auspicious:
While ascending and descending on your journey   285
seek one whose values are your own
Yu and Tang sought men as stern as them
finding Gao Yao and Zhi enabled them to rule.
As long as your heart is set on beauty
what need do you have for a go-between   290
when Fu Yue was building walls at Fuyan
Wu Ding didn't doubt he could use him.
Seeing Lu Wang pounding knives
King Wen made him his minister

---

[279] A shaman using this name appears as early as the Shang dynasty. The spirits such shamans channel can remain active for hundreds, even thousands, of years. Xian is also the name of the thirty-first hexagram of the *Yijing* and denotes harmony between a man and a woman.

[282] This is the mountain where Emperor Shun's grave is located.

[285] Referring to the ascent and descent of a shaman.

[288] As noted earlier, Yu and Tang founded the Xia and Shang dynasties. Gao Yao was Yu's chief minister, and Zhi (aka Yi Yin) was Tang's.

[291] Fu Yue was a convict laborer. Wu Ding was a Shang dynasty king (d. 1192 BCE) and was credited with the use of rammed-earth walls.

[293] Lu Wang, aka Jiang Ziya, was a butcher. King Wen (r. 1152–1122 BCE) of the Zhou dynasty made him his prime minister.

hearing Ning Qi sing 295
Duke Huan made him his adviser.
Even though the year isn't late
and the season not yet over
the cuckoo could start calling soon
and sweet-smelling plants lose their scent. 300
No matter how splendid your sash
the crowd of weeds will obscure it
and the more unforgiving at court
will destroy it out of envy.
In such a chaotic world in flux 305
how could I remain any longer
orchid and angelica had lost their fragrance
sweet flag and cymbidium had become mere grasses.
Where were the sweet-smelling plants of the past
wormwood and mugwort were all that remained 310
what other reason could there be
than the death of the love of beauty.
I thought I could rely on orchid
but he was untrue and mere appearance
he gave up beauty to fit in with the crowd 315

---

[295] When Duke Huan (r. 685–643 BCE) of the state of Qi heard Ning Qi singing, he made him his chief adviser.

[299] Because the cuckoo's seasonal range is among the greatest of all birds, it announces the end of spring in North China, and in Central China, where this poem was written, it announces the beginning of autumn.

[310] *Artemisia absinthium* and *Artemisia argyi*.

as long as he could rank as a fragrant plant.
Pepper had gone from flattery to contempt
all dogwood wanted was to fill sachets
insinuating themselves in order to advance
how could such plants be respected?   320
Of course it was the current of the times
who could avoid its changes
I watched this happen to pepper and orchid
not to mention gooseneck and lovage.
I would have changed too had I cast aside beauty   325
this sash was all that I treasured
its fragrance never left me
its scent never failed me.
Adjusting my ways to please myself
I shall wander in search of a mate   330
while my adornments are in their prime
I shall travel the world searching high and low.
Having heard the oracle foretell my fortune
I prepared to leave on an auspicious day
for an offering I broke off jade twigs   335

---

[329] Unlike Qu Yuan's first spirit journey, which began with a blaze of light, this time he expects to have some control over where and how he travels, and he makes preparations.

[333] Referring to "Two beauties are a certain match" (line 259).

[335] Trees made of jade were said to grow in the Kunlun Mountains. Although Qu Yuan isn't there yet, the use of jade and other minerals was common in Daoist elixirs.

and ground the best ones for provisions.
I yoked winged dragons for my steeds
fashioned a chariot of ivory and jade
so two hearts might become one
I shall leave on a distant journey. 340
The destination I chose was Kunlun
a road that disappeared into the distance
my cloud banners darkened the sky
my jade-white phoenixes called.
I left in the morning from the Ford of Heaven 345
by nightfall I reached the Western Border
pennants on the wings of my phoenixes
flapped in the air high above me.
I traveled quickly past the Shifting Sands
then leisurely along the Red River 350

[337] The "winged dragons" and "jade-white phoenixes" (line 344) refer to his horses.

[339] Again, referring to the oracle's declaration.

[340] Though he has no guide, Qu Yuan has a destination in mind.

[341] The Kunlun Mountains have long been connected with the origin of Chinese culture and its shamanic tradition. See also the note to line 372 and the note to Tao Yuanming's poem 24.

[345] Referring to a group of nine stars in Cygnus that span the Milky Way and form the bridge that allows separated lovers to meet.

[346] The western border of the Chinese world, but not the known world.

[349] Located in the Kunlun Mountains.

[350] A river whose source is in the Kunlun Mountains.

I instructed water dragons to form a bridge
then ordered the Western Lord to help me cross.
Since the road was long and hard
I told my carriages to fly ahead
to go past the Buzhou Mountains then south   355
and to meet me at the Western Sea.
With a thousand more in my train
jade hub to jade hub we rode forth
our dragon teams surging ahead
our cloud banners twisting like snakes.   360
Restraining myself I controlled my pace
in the distance spirits filled the sky
I paused there all day for pleasure
performing the Nine Songs and Shao Dances.
Ascending toward the great light above   365
suddenly I looked down on familiar lands
my groom sighed and my horses whinnied
having turned to look they wouldn't continue.
Alas in this land where none understands me

[352] A name given to the legendary third-millennium BCE ruler Shao Hao, who was said to rule over the Western Heavens. Qu Yuan is no longer traveling as a mere mortal but as a king on his way to his kingdom.

[355] Identified with the Pamirs, northwest of the Kunlun Mountains.

[356] Perhaps the Caspian Sea, visited by King Mu circa 950 BCE.

[364] The Nine Songs are shamanistic elegies praising the virtues of Yu the Great. The music known as Shao was composed by Emperor Shun.

why should I care for its ancient capital   370
since no one is able to govern with beauty
I shall go where Peng and Xian dwell.

[372] The *Shanhaijing,* or Book of Mountains and Waters—which was appa-
rently composed during Qu Yuan's lifetime—says both Peng and Xian
retired to the Kunlun Mountains to practice occult arts. According to the
early second century commentary of Wang Yi, Peng Xian was the name
of an official who lived in the second millennium BCE and committed
suicide by drowning. This is the source of the tradition that interprets
Qu Yuan's meaning here as a declaration of his intent to commit suicide.
However, no support has ever been found for Wang Yi's claim, and every-
thing in this poem argues against such an interpretation.

Tao Yuanming

Tao Yuanming 陶渊明

If everyone in China who said Tao Yuanming was their favorite poet lined up, the line might be longer than the Great Wall. It's not just his poetry people love, it's the man. In "East of Town," Wei Yingwu said, "Someday I'll retire and build a hut / to be like Old Tao would be sweet." In another poem, titled "In Imitation of Tao Pengze," Wei took on his persona: "At sunset I sit down with farmers / under thatched eaves all of us drunk / life is about more than plenty." Tao's poetry wasn't just poetry. It was an expression of his decision to live his life according to his understanding of the Dao— poverty be damned. How could anyone not invite him in for a drink?

As for his life, Tao Yuanming was born in 365 in the town of Chaisang, or Xunyang, or Jiangzhou, depending on whether you're talking about the administrative center for the county, the prefecture, or the province. They were all located within a few hundred meters of each other on the south shore of the middle reaches of the Yangzi, just upstream from where the river is joined by the waters of Poyanghu, China's largest freshwater lake.

The most significant figure in Yuanming's life was his great-grandfather Tao Kan 陶侃, who was born at the south end of the lake. Tao Kan grew up as poor as poor could be, but he became one of the great martial artists and military figures of his time. Among his exploits was rescuing the Jin dynasty court from its besieged capital of Luoyang near the banks of the Yellow River and ensuring its safe relocation to Nanjing on the Yangzi. With such an ancestor, Yuanming could have had any kind of life he wanted, and he chose to farm—though not at first.

Being a good son, in his thirties he tried his hand at a career. Since his heroes included the ancient sages who were guided by their understanding of the Dao, Yuanming tried to do what he could to help manifest that in public service. His first attempt didn't last a month, and he should have stopped with that. The pretension that such jobs required was simply too much for him. Still, he had a family with, eventually, eight mouths to feed, and so a few years later, he agreed to serve as an aide to the two most powerful men in the country: first to Huan Xuan 桓玄, then to Liu Yu 劉裕—both of whom later deposed Jin emperors and established their own dynasties. If anyone was governing according to the Dao, Tao Yuanming certainly didn't see any evidence of it. It's a wonder that he lasted nearly three years with Huan Xuan. He was saved by the death of his mother, which required a period of mourning.

When the mourning period ended two years later, Yuanming also served as adviser to Liu Yu, who quickly put an end to Huan Xuan's short-lived Huan Chu dynasty. Yuanming declined further service at the highest level and thought he would try something on a smaller stage. He accepted the job of magistrate of Pengze on the far shore of Poyanghu. Again, as soon as he arrived, he couldn't wait to quit. This time he was rescued by the death of his sister. After serving less than ninety days, he packed his bags, rowed home, and never served again. He spent the last two decades of his life as a farmer. It wasn't easy. Farming never is. He often went to bed hungry. But there was no turning back. Rather than bow to those he didn't respect or rely on the legacy of his famous ancestor, he chose to support his family by working the land—for the most part by himself, it seems. His mother's mother and father's father were both children of Tao Kan, and his own five sons all demonstrated various intellectual disabilities—not that Yuanming ever blamed his hardships on anyone but himself.

As for the principles by which he lived, Tao Yuanming has often been thought of as a Confucian. Most officials were. But his hero wasn't Confucius—not that he didn't respect the teachings of the great sage. He felt such teachings were meant for another time—ten emperors ascended the throne in Nanjing, two of whom were murdered, during his six decades. Some have even suggested he was a Buddhist. After all, among his closest friends was Master Huiyuan 慧遠, one of the most famous Buddhist monks in China. But liking Huiyuan didn't make him a Buddhist. He loved to read, and he admired such Daoist writers as Zhuangzi, but he wasn't a Daoist either, not a Daoist Daoist. He took his lessons from all three traditions, but mainly from the Dao of his own life. His hero was a farmer who laughed at Confucius, then disappeared into the mist with his hoe. Yuanming decided to do the same.

Fortunately, when the farm work was done, Yuanming wrote poems and shared them with friends. Depending on how you count those that survived, we have one hundred fifty-two under fifty-nine titles. That wasn't a lot. But he wasn't famous for his poetry when he was alive; he was famous for the way he lived. He was a recluse, the most famous member of the Three Recluses of Chaisang, as they were called in the capital. When the governor once asked if he might pay a visit, Yuanming turned him down—not that he didn't attend the occasional celebration involving friends who were officials. And certainly he was only too happy to join any neighbor with enough wine to share. He wasn't a hermit, he was a recluse—an affable, well-read man who wanted nothing to do with pretense.

It's noteworthy that scholars still disagree whether his poem "Begging for Food" was written when he was twenty-one or just before he died, at the age of sixty-two. Poverty dogged his life. It isn't that he wanted to be poor; it was that doing without was the inevitable companion to his determination to live the life he lived. For him, that meant enduring poverty. There was, though, one thing he wished he could have changed. In 427, two months before he died, in one of his "Pallbearer Songs" he wrote, "I only regret while I was alive / I didn't get more wine." I wish I could have been his neighbor.

from *Choosing to Be Simple*

1   Stilling the Passions

Earlier, Zhang Heng wrote "Calming the Passions" and Cai Yong "Quieting the Passions" in language that was restrained and unadorned. While they began by stirring the imagination, they ended in simple elegance, thereby suppressing unbridled or vulgar thoughts and providing what might help serve as a warning. Writers of subsequent generations have continued to elaborate and expand on this theme. In this village of gardens, I have lots of spare time and have once more wet my brush. Though what I have written isn't that profound, perhaps it hasn't missed my intent.

How captivating her appearance
incomparable and rare
her beauty could topple a kingdom
yet she wanted to be known for virtue
her purity was like that of a clear jade pendant
her fragrance like an orchid in the woods
she cherished the most ordinary things
yet her aspirations rivaled the clouds
she grieved when dawn turned to dusk
she was moved our lives are all toil

---

[1] Written in 383 at the family home in Chaisang when Yuanming was nineteen.

that they end in less than a hundred years
that our cares outnumber our joys
she lifted the red curtain and sat erect
playing the zither was her passion
her slender fingers conveyed her feelings
her white sleeves flashed through the air
suddenly her lovely eyes glanced
as if she might laugh or speak.
Before the tune was half over
sunlight filled the west window
her mournful notes echoed through the woods
clouds rested on the hills,
she looked up at the patterns in the sky
then down and tightened the strings
her spirit and manner were enchanting
moving or still she was graceful.
The delicate notes she played entranced me
I wanted to draw near her and speak
I wanted to express my intentions
but feared I would be breaking a rule*
I looked for a phoenix to take my message
worried another would precede me
perplexed and disconcerted
suddenly my spirit was transported
I was the collar of her shirt
inhaling the scent of her silken hair

*Establishing relationships was usually done through go-betweens.

sadly when she disrobed at bedtime
I lamented the length of autumn nights.
I was the belt of her skirt
tied around her lithesome body
but I sighed at the changing seasons
when she changed her clothes too.
I was the oil in her hair
as she leaned and brushed her dark locks
but I winced whenever she washed it
then rinsed and dried it in the sun.
I was the mascara on her brows
following the idle movements of her eyes
sadly makeup needs refreshing
and it's smeared when it's applied.
I was the woven grass in her mat
pressing against her body through the fall
then replaced by something thicker
and not seeing her again until next year.
I was the silk in her slippers
touching her pale feet as she walked
sadly she walked but also rested
and cast them aside before her bed.
I was her shadow during the day
with her no matter where she went
but sadly in the shade of trees
alas we had to part.
I was her candle during the night
lighting her fair face in her pillared room

sadly when the sun spread its rays
my light once eclipsed was extinguished.
I was the bamboo of her fan
wafting cool breezes in her gentle hand
until the dew of autumn appeared
and I watched her from her distant sleeve.
I was a plank of paulownia wood*
a singing zither across her knees
but music can reach a point where it's sad
suddenly she stopped and laid me down.
Seeing all my wishes denied
all my valiant efforts in vain
and no one to console me
I wandered in the woods to the south
I stopped beneath a magnolia wet with dew
then in the shade of a pine
thinking I might see her I walked on
joy and fear mingled in my heart.
When she didn't appear I felt lost
having failed in my quest I was depressed
I gathered my thin robe and returned to the path
looking at the sunset I kept sighing
my steps were pointless and in vain
I felt dismayed and dejected
leaves fluttered from the trees
the air was cool and turning colder

*The wood of the paulownia tree is prized for its lightness and tone.

my shadow vanished as the sun set
the crescent moon lit the edges of the clouds
with a sad cry a bird returned alone
searching for its mate another didn't
sadly my youthful years were fading
and I hated to see this one ending
in my dreams I looked for her that night
my spirit felt adrift and apprehensive
like a boatman without an oar
or a climber without a handhold.
Winter stars filled my window
the north wind was chilly
I was restless and couldn't sleep
my thoughts wandered all night.
I tied my sash and rose to greet the dawn
heavy frost glittered on the steps
the roosters hadn't yet crowed
in the distance I heard a shrill flute
with a subtle harmony at first
then ending harsh and mournful.
Thinking it was she
I asked a passing cloud to convey my feelings.
The cloud left without a word
it drifted then disappeared
the more I thought the sadder I became
blocked in the end by mountains and rivers
I called on the breeze to end my malaise
I sent my feeble hopes home on the waves

upset at my tryst among the vines*
I sang some lines from a Shaonan song
once I calmed down my heart was still there
my feelings now dwelt beyond the horizon.

*In the *Shijing* (94), "Vines in the Wild" is about a boy and girl meeting by chance. In Tao's day, such trysts were considered illicit. The book's Shaonan section was said to present love in a proper setting.

4 Held Up at Guilin by Winds While Returning from the Capital in the Fifth Month of 400

I

Pressing ahead retracing our route
I was counting the days to behold my old home
first I'll be happy to wait on my mother
then I'll be glad to see my brothers
poling our way through a tortuous course
I pointed to the light fading in the west
what river or mountain holds no danger
a son returning home thinks of what lies ahead
the wind from the south betrayed us
stuck in a side channel we shipped our oars
surrounded by a sea of tall grass
what few trees there were were far apart
someone said we still had far to go
more than a hundred *li*
straining my eyes I could see South Mountain
all I could do was sigh

4.i Written in 400. Tao was heading up the Yangzi to Jiangling, where he served as an aide to Huan Xuan, and planned to stop on the way in Chaisang to see his family. South Mountain refers to Lushan, which was just south of his home.

II

People sigh about the hardships of travel
I'm just learning about them now
about the size of mountains and rivers
and the unexpected dangers of both
about crashing waves that echo across the sky
and relentless winds that never cease
the more I travel the more I long for home
why am I stuck where I am
I've been thinking how much I love my garden
and why haven't I said goodbye to the world
how long will my good years last
and why did I ever question my heart

4.ii Tao's first post lasted less than a month. He turned down the second
one. This one, in Jiangling, where he served as an adviser to the warlord
Huan Xuan, lasted from 398 to the fall of 401. It turned out to be his only
real job.

5 Traveling past Tukou at Night While Returning to Jiangling in the Seventh Month of 401 after My Leave

For thirty years I stayed at home
ignorant of the world's goings-on
my loves were poetry and history
I had no ambition beyond my garden
why did I leave it all behind
for distant Jingzhou in the west
part from friends at the river
slap oars beneath a new autumn moon
as a cold wind rose at dusk
the night sky was clear and bright
what glimmered in the vault of heaven
shimmered on the surface of the river
thinking about my mission I couldn't sleep
still traveling alone at night
I never cared for Shang songs
I'd rather stick with farming
toss my hat and go back to the village
not work for a salary or rank
cultivate something real in a hut
perhaps become known for something good

[5] Written in the summer of 401 while traveling again on the Yangzi. After taking leave to visit his sick mother in Chaisang, Tao was returning upriver to Jiangling (Jingzhou) and the court of Huan Xuan, who would soon be usurping the throne. Tao's mother's death three months later gave him the excuse he was looking for to quit while he could. "Shang songs" were often sung when looking for a job.

8 In Early Spring of 403, Thinking of Ancient Farmers

I

I heard we had fields to the south
but never went when I was young
once people find themselves hungry
they can't avoid the whip of spring
I hitched my cart before dawn
on the road I was lost in thought
birds welcomed the new season
warmer air meant good things to come
winter bamboo had nearly covered the path
it was far and people were few
this was why the old man with his staff
disappeared and didn't return
his understanding shamed men of learning
what protected him wasn't superficial

[8.i] Written in 403 in the village of Shangjingli. After two years of mourning, Tao decided to follow the men he admired and take up farming. In the village outside Chaisang where he relocated during the mourning period, he had a garden and a few fruit trees but no fields. Still, his parents owned some land to the south, between Shangjingli and Lushan. This was his first experience of clearing and plowing land. The "old man with his staff" was a hermit who asked Zilu what kind of master Confucius was if he didn't teach his disciples farming. When Confucius heard about their exchange, he sent Zilu to talk to the man, but the man had left. Zilu is then quoted as saying, "The superior man serves in office and follows what is right even if he knows that the Way is not being followed." (*Lunyu* 18.7)

II

Teachers of the past left lessons
worry about the Way not poverty
considering this beyond my reach
I set my heart on toil instead
I was glad it was time to grab a plow
I smiled and urged my fellow farmers on
the fields finally felt fresh air
sprouts too thought of becoming new
even if the harvest wasn't certain
the work was mostly a pleasure
the plowing and planting were done
no one stopped to ask directions
at sunset we went home together
and I troubled my neighbors for some wine
singing a poem I closed my door
a man of terraced fields for now

[8.ii] "Worry about the way not poverty": Quoted from Confucius, *Lunyu* 15.32. The famous dictum near the beginning of the Confucian text known as the *Daxue* (Great Learning)—"If you can be new / be new every day / be new again today"—inspired Ezra Pound to make it his rallying cry. Confucius asked his disciple to ask some recluses who were farming about the location of "the ford" (*Lunyu* 18.6). The land Tao's family owned to the south was in the hills and required terracing. It would have been too much trouble for anyone but the poorest of farmers or a recluse—men Tao not only admires but with whom he now identifies.

19 Returning to My Garden and Fields

I was socially awkward when I was young
I preferred hills and mountains instead
by mistake I fell into a net of illusions
I was gone for thirteen years
but a bird on a tether longs for the woods
and a fish in a pond recalls the old depths
so I cleared some land in the hills south of town
choosing to be simple I came back to farm
my property includes more than three acres
my thatch house is maybe nine mats wide
elms and willows shade the eaves in back
fruit trees spread before the door
the nearest town is off in the haze
smoke hangs above the village houses
a dog barks in a distant lane
a cock crows atop a mulberry tree
there's no dust or trash in my yard
my house is empty but filled with peace
no longer imprisoned in a cage
I'm back again and I'm free

[19] Written in 406 in Shangjingli—the first of five poems written upon returning home after quitting his final job. Shangjingli was located a few kilometers outside the southwest corner of Chaisang. Mats were typically three feet wide. Hence, his house would have been about twenty-seven feet on a side—just big enough for him and his wife and six kids—and elsewhere he mentions a houseboy.

24　On Reading the Book of Mountains and Waters

The first month of summer and all that grows is tall
the trees have surrounded my house with leaves
birds are glad to have a place to roost
I love this hut of mine too
having finished the plowing and planting
I've returned to my books again
such a remote lane doesn't see many ruts
it tends to deter even the carts of friends
I'm happy with a cup of spring wine
and vegetables from my garden
and the lightest of rains from the east
and with it a welcome breeze
I skimmed the Tale of King Mu
and glanced at the pictures in Mountains and Waters
having surveyed the whole world
how can I not be pleased

[24] Written in 407 at his home in Shangjingli, the first of thirteen poems. The Book of Mountains and Waters (*Shanhaijing* 山海經) was a shaman's guide to the geography of China dating back to the early first millennium BCE—and it included pictures. The Tale of King Mu (*Mutianzijuan* 穆王子傳) was the journal of King Mu (d. 933 BCE) of the Zhou dynasty and recounts his travels in Central Asia as far as the Caspian Sea. His journey was considered to be a myth until a copy was discovered in a tomb in 281 CE. The tomb belonged to King Xiang of Wei and was sealed in 318 BCE.

26 In the Sixth Month of 408, Encountering Fire

For a thatched hut in a forgotten lane
I was happy to trade a painted carriage
but a fierce wind rose this summer
the trees and house suddenly caught fire
not even the roof remained
we took shelter in a boat just outside the gate
in the vastness of early autumn dusk
beneath the distant waxing moon
vegetables are starting to grow again
but birds are too frightened to return
late last night standing lost in thought
I surveyed the four quarters of the sky
since coming of age I have held my course
suddenly forty years are gone
my body has accepted the changes
but my spirit has remained unmoved
consisting of something solid and true
it's harder than jade or stone
I think back to Donghu times
when surplus grain was left in the fields
people patted their bellies and had no concerns
they rose at dawn and retired at dusk
because this isn't that time
I'm watering our garden now

26 Written in the early fall of 408 in Shangjiingli. "Donghu times" was a
legendary golden age.

28 The Ninth Day of the Ninth Month of 409

The last traces of autumn have faded
a cold wind has joined the dew
the climbing vines have stopped blooming
the leaves are all gone from the trees
since the cooler weather cleared the air
the edge of heaven looks higher
sadly the sound of cicadas is gone
replaced by that of passing geese
the ten thousand changes are all different
as if our lives weren't hard enough
since ancient times we appear then vanish
the thought of this burned me inside
in order to relieve such feelings
I drank some wine and felt happy
I don't know about a thousand years
just let me prolong this day

[28] Written in 409 shortly after moving to West Hut. After trying to live in a houseboat, Tao moved here, where the land was suitable for slash-and-burn dry rice farming and apparently better to farm than the land the family owned south of Shangjingli. The move here would have occurred early enough in the spring to plant. Rome was sacked by the Visigoths the following year.

33   Lament for My Cousin Zhongde

Visiting your old home I controlled my grief
the tears were in response to my heart
you ask whom I grieve for
it's the one I love now in the dark
the robe I'm wearing is required of cousins
but our feelings were those of brothers
when I last held your hand at the gate
how could I know you'd die first
a destiny none of us escapes
your dreams left unfinished
your mother ill with grief
your children under ten
two tablets in an empty room
no sound of crying day or night
dust covering your vacant seat
last year's grass taking over your yard
no trace of your footsteps on the paths
only memories among the flowers and trees
your transformation gone like smoke
your form never seen again
as I slowly retraced my steps
my heart was weighed down by grief

---

[33] Written in late spring of 412 in Shangjingli. Tao's cousin died in the eighth month of the previous year. "Two tablets" implies the cousin's wife died first and that her spirit tablet was already in the room.

36 Exchanging Poems with Liu of Chaisang

Few people visit such a poor place
sometimes I forget about the seasons
until village yards are covered with leaves
and sadly I realize it's autumn
even with sunflowers lighting the north window
and grain nodding in our fields to the south
still I can't feel happy
wondering if I'll have another year
I tell my wife to bring the children
it's a perfect day for a hike

41 Drinking Wine

I built my hut beside a path
but hear no cart or horse
you ask how can this be
where the mind goes I go too
picking chrysanthemums by the eastern fence
in the distance I see South Mountain
the mountain air the sunset light
birds flying home together
in this there is a truth
I'd explain if I could remember the words

---

[36] Written in 414 in Shangjingli to Tao's fellow recluse Liu Yimin.

[41] Written in 417 in Shangjingli, the fifth of twenty poems inspired by wine.

45　Double Ninth, Living Retired

Since retiring, I have come to love the name Double Ninth. Although fall chrysanthemums fill my garden, I have no means to get any wine. Swallowing the flowers of the Ninth in vain, I put my feelings into words.

Our wishes have always outnumbered our days
naturally we prefer to live longer
whenever this day and month align
everyone loves to hear this name
when the dew is cold and summer winds are gone
when the air is clear and the stars are bright
when there isn't any trace of sparrows
and we begin to hear geese
it's wine that can end our cares
and chrysanthemums that can free us from old age
what can a gentleman in a thatched hut do
helplessly watching the season go by
embarrassed by a dry cup and an empty jug
and winter flowers blooming in vain
I pull my robe tighter and sing to myself
and recall long-forgotten feelings
living retired certainly has its joys
and living longer isn't without its merits

45 Written in the fall of 419 in Shangjingli. As explained at Wei Yingwu's poem 1, on Double Ninth—nine being a *yang* number—men celebrate their longevity.

60 Pallbearer Songs

I

Whatever is born must die
sooner doesn't mean a lesser fate
last night like any other man
this morning I'm listed among the dead
where did my breath and spirit go
leaving a shriveled form in a coffin
children crying for their father
friends touching me in tears
never again to know success or failure
or to distinguish right from wrong
ten thousand autumns from now
who will know of my glory or shame
I only regret while I was alive
I didn't get more wine

II

In the past I often had nothing to drink
today my cup is full in vain
spring wine has begun to ferment
but when will I taste it again

[60] Written in the ninth month of 427 in Shangjingli, two months before
Tao died. Rice wine normally takes a month or so to ferment, but the
longer the better.

a table of dishes is laid out before me
relatives and friends cry at my side
I try to speak but my lips don't move
I try to look but my eyes are blank
I slept beneath a roof in the past
I'll be spending tonight in the weeds
once they carry me out the door
I won't be coming back again

III

Where weeds are boundless
where poplars sough
in the heavy frost of fall
I'll be carried far from town
in all directions no sign of a house
nothing but the tops of mounds
the horses will neigh at the sky
the wind will make a mournful sound
once the crypt is closed
I won't see dawn for a thousand years
a thousand years no dawn
all that I've learned of no use
those who came to see me off
will go back to their families
relatives might grieve for a while
others will already be singing
once we're dead what's there to say
our bodies become one with the hills

Dancing with the Dead

Dancing with the Dead: Language, Poetry, and the Art of Translation

Every time I translate a book of poems, I learn a new way of dancing. The people with whom I dance, though, are the dead, not the recently departed, but people who have been dead a long time. A thousand years or so seems about right. And the music has to be Chinese. It's the only music I've learned to dance to.

I'm not sure what led me to this conclusion, that translation is like dancing. Buddhist meditation. Language theory. Cognitive psychology. Drugs. Sex. Rock and roll. My ruminations on the subject go back more than twenty-five years to when I was first living in Taiwan.* One day I was browsing through the pirated editions at Caves Books in Taipei, and I picked up a copy, in English, of Allen Ginsberg's *Howl*. It was like trying to make sense of hieroglyphs. I put it back down and looked for something else. Then a friend loaned me a video of Ginsberg reading *Howl*. What a difference. In Ginsberg's voice, I heard the energy and rhythm, the sound and the silence, the vision, the poetry. The same thing happened when I read some of Gary Snyder's poems, then heard him read. The words on a page,

* In October 2004, I delivered this short piece at the International Chinese Poetry Conference held in Boston at Simmons University (formerly Simmons College), organized and hosted by Afaa Weaver.

I concluded, are not the poem. They are the recipe, not the meal—steps drawn on a dance floor, not the dance.

For the past hundred thousand years or so, we human beings have developed language as our primary means of communication—first spoken language and more recently written language. We have used language to convey information to each other, to communicate. But there is a set of questions just below the surface that we prefer not to address. How well does language do what we think it does? And what does it do? The reason we prefer not to address such questions is that language is so mercurial. We can never quite pin it down. It is forever in flux. And it is forever in flux because we, its speakers and writers and translators, are forever in flux. We can't step into the same thought twice. We might use or read or hear the same word twice, but how can it mean the same thing if the person who uses or reads or hears that word is not the same person? We speak of language as if it were a fixed phenomenon, and we teach it and learn it as if it were carved in stone. But it is more like water, because we are more like water. Language is at the surface of the much deeper flux that is our riverine minds. Thus, if we approach translation by focusing on language alone, we mistake the waves for the river, the tracks for the journey.

But this isn't all. A number of linguists and anthropologists are of the opinion that language was developed by early humans not simply for the purpose of communication but for deception. All beings communicate with each other, but at least on this planet only humans deceive each other. And for such deception, we rely primarily on language. It isn't easy for us to hide our feelings and intentions in our facial or bodily expressions, but language offers ready and endless opportunities for altering and manipulating the truth. Thus, the question for a translator is not only the efficiency of language but also its truthfulness. That is, does it actually do what we think it does, and does what it does have any basis other than in fiction?

We live in worlds of linguistic fabrication. Pine trees do not grow with the word *pine* hanging from their branches. Nor does a pine tree "welcome" anyone to its shade. It is we who decide what words to use, and, like Alice, what they mean. And what they mean does not necessarily have anything to do with reality. They are sleights of the mind as well as of the hand and lips. And if we mistake words for reality, they are no longer simply sleights but lies. And yet, if we can see them for what they are, if we can see beyond their deception, they are like so many crows on the wing, disappearing with the setting sun into the trees beyond our home. This is what poetry does. It brings us closer to the truth. Not *to* the truth, for language wilts in such light, but close enough to feel the heat.

According to the Great Preface to the *Book of Poetry,* the Chinese character for poetry means "words from the heart." This would seem to be a characteristic of poetry in other cultures as well—that it comes from the heart, unlike prose, which comes from the head. Thus, prose retains the deceptive quality of language, while poetry is our ancient and ongoing attempt to transcend language, to overcome its deceptive nature by exploring and exposing the deeper levels of our consciousness and emotions. Though poetry is still mediated by language, it involves a minimal use of words, and it also weakens the dominance of language through such elements as sound and silence, rhythm and harmony, elements more common to music than logic. In poetry, we come as close as we are likely to get to the meaning and to the heart of another.

This, too, isn't all. Poetry is not simply "words from the heart." A poet doesn't make a poem so much as discover a poem, maybe in a garden or a ghetto, maybe in a garbage dump or a government corridor, or in a galaxy of stars. In poetry, we go beyond ourselves to the heart of the universe, where we might be moved by something as small as a grain of sand or as great as the Ganges.

So what does all this mean for the translator? For me it means that I cannot simply limit myself to the words I find on the page. I have to go deeper, to dive into the river. If language is our greatest collective lie, poetry is our attempt to undo that deception. When I translate a poem, I don't think of the Chinese on the page as the poem, only evidence of the existence of a poem. Poetry shows itself in words, and words are how we know it. But words are only the surface. Even after poets give their discoveries expression in language, they continue to discover a poem's deeper nuances, and they make changes: maybe a few words, maybe a few lines, maybe much more. The poem, as I see it, is a never-ending process of discovery. And it isn't just language. It's the unspoken vision that impels a poet and to which the poet tries to give expression. But the poet never gives complete expression to that vision, only a few fragments from a kaleidoscopic insight, a few steps on the dance floor impelled by music even the poet hears only imperfectly.

Then a translator comes along, and things change. It is only then that the poet no longer dances alone but with a partner. And together they manifest a deeper insight into the poem, into the music that motivates the dance. Thus, I have come to realize that translation is not just another literary art, it is the ultimate literary art, the ultimate challenge in understanding as well as performance. For me, this means a tango with Li Bai, a waltz with Wei Yingwu, a dance with the dead.

About Red Pine

Bill Porter assumes the pen name Red Pine for his translation work. He was born in Los Angeles in 1943, grew up in the Idaho Panhandle, served a tour of duty in the US Army, graduated from the University of California with a degree in anthropology, and attended graduate school at Columbia University. Uninspired by the prospect of an academic career, he dropped out of Columbia and moved to a Buddhist monastery in Taiwan. His translations have been honored with a number of awards, including two NEA translation fellowships, a Guggenheim Fellowship, a PEN Translation Prize, and the inaugural Asian Literature Award of the American Literary Translators Association. Porter received the 2018 Thornton Wilder Prize for Translation bestowed by the American Academy of Arts and Letters. He lives in Port Townsend, Washington.

Donors to the Publication

Zeinab Masud Agha

Anonymous

Jane & Michael Armstrong

Marian Birch and Bronson
West

Jeffrey Bishop

Susan Biskeborn and Tom
Richardson

Elsa Bowman

Brant Brechbiel

David Brewster and Mary Kay
Sneeringer

Deborah Buchanan and Scott
Teitsworth

Vincent Buck

Colleen Chartier and Richard
Andrews

Andrew Chen and Rebekah
Green

Christopher

Peter Clifford and Laura
Saunders

Marty Cole and Ki Gottberg

Linda Corbett

Christopher Corkery

Leslie Cox

Nicholas Croft

Gil Cuadra and Stephanie
Nguyen

In honor of Garth Culver

In memory of Walter Daspit III

Jacob Dirr

Malcolm Dorn

Barbara Droker

John Feins

Kenneth Fosse

Jerry Fulks

Mimi Gardner Gates

Fleur Green

Maria Gunn

Art and Mary Ann Hanlon,
in honor of Sam Hamill

Scott Hanson

Jean Harrington

James Houlahan

Tiina Jaatinen

Rob Jacques

Ron Janssen

Julie Christine Johnson

Kenneth Jones

Sheila Khalov

Mary and Allan Kollar,
in honor of Rocky

Michael and Lisa Lackey

Chris La Tray

Kris and Paul Leathers

Jim Lenfestey

Michael Levin and Carol Schapira

Peter Lewis and Johnna Turiano

Ralph J. Long Jr.
Maria C. Mackey
The team at Make It Matter
Larry Mawby and Lois Bahle
Margaret D. McGee
Janet McInerney
The McKee Clan
Elisabeth Mention
Ibrahim Moussa
Ned Mudd and Joyce Hudson
In honor of our first-born grandson, Henry Bergstrom (Mountain Stream) Musto
Jennifer and Jamie Newton
Chris and Kami Niehoff
Allen K. Nishikawa
Walter Parsons
Robert Petersen
Bob Phillips
Madelyn S. Pitts
Sue Raley
Emily and Dan Raymond
Bruce Redwine
Renata's Mom and Dad
Tripp and Sara Ritter
Bethany M. Rodenhuis
Larry Rouch
Hal Rowe
Pamela Jean Sampel

Joanne and Gil Schoefer
Scott
Kelley and Philip Swanstrom
Shaw
Liesl Slabaugh and Joseph Bednarik
William Slaughter
Byron Springer
Elliott Starks
Roger Dale Stude
Sam Sudar
George and Kim Suyama
Laura Lewis Thayer and James Ward
Jody and Jim Thomson
In memory of Tsering Rinpoche and Khyonla Rinpoche
Chase Twichell
Steve Voorhees
Dan Waggoner
Margaret H. Wagner
Scott Walker
Church of Tarkus Minister General Jack Wells II (FT), in memory of Marjorie and Jack Wells, Grace and Donald Hiscox, Ruth Berven, et al.
D.D. Wigley
Brooke Williams

Poetry is vital to language and living. Since 1972, Copper Canyon Press has published extraordinary poetry from around the world to engage the imaginations and intellects of readers, writers, booksellers, librarians, teachers, students, and donors.

WE ARE GRATEFUL FOR THE MAJOR SUPPORT PROVIDED BY:

academy of
american poets

THE PAUL G. ALLEN
FAMILY FOUNDATION

amazon *literary*
partnership ❧

4
CULTURE

the **point**
envision·enact·evolve

Lannan

△ ▼▼▼
ART WORKS.

**National
Endowment
for the Arts**
arts.gov

WASHINGTON STATE
ARTS COMMISSION

A&
OFFICE OF ARTS & CULTURE
SEATTLE

**The Witter Bynner Foundation
for Poetry**